52 WEEKS TO BETTER WRITING

I0455506

52 Weeks to Better Writing
Table of Contents

Publisher Note

This book was written as my own self-education guide between 2005 and 2007. It was a work of experimentation and I can only hope that it can help somebody. It is not organized in any particular fashion but instead the sections were written and left in the order that they arose in my quest to become a writer. I am still on the journey and I hope this book can help you along your own. Any comments can be sent to evenflow111@gmail.com

                                        - Roger Newman

52 Weeks to Better Writing
by Roger Newman

Good writing is a process that must be learned. It is not something that we automatically have a gift for unless we are lucky. Most of us have to work to be able to write well. This course is about learning one how to be a good writer. It is about process. But just like any skill it is a process that can be learned.

This course is designed to teach you to be a better writer. Whether your goal is writing the great American novel or simply contributing an article to your company's newsletters, you will find that this course will help you reach that objective in a manner that ensures readers will get your message and enjoy the process.

Most people learn the process of writing by trial and error. However, this process is fraught with problems. The first of which is the fact that the audience you are exposing your writing too may not be the one that is appropriate. This course goes beyond all of that and focuses on key principles and techniques you can use to ensure that you writing is well read and enjoyed. There are no shortcuts though and there is a certain amount of work involved in order to reach competency.

Throughout the course you will find reference to those who are attempting to write books. While we realize this may not be the case for everybody it will help if you imagine that to be the case. The only difference between an article and a book is in scope. One is simply an expansion of the other. Therefore, thinking in terms of a book length manuscript may help you in visualizing the finished project that you are working with. The same principles apply no matter the length.

Another caveat to this course is that the objective is to get your writing to a level that it has an audience. An audience may be your fellow employees or people who pay money for your writing. Either way the person who reads the end product is your audience. It will help to constantly keep your audience in mind as you are writing.   It will help you to make decisions that will improve the final product.

We will begin the course as if you are new to writing.   If you are not then simply pretend that you are and play along to get maximum value out of the course.   Those of you who have been writing for a long time will invariably find valuable advice if you can set aside your judgments of what information is below you.   Simply listen and learn and see where it takes you.

As with all 52 Week courses we recognize that our beliefs dictate our results. Thus, we will go about setting some preliminary beliefs that will empower you and ensure your success through the remainder of the course.   The ten core beliefs of this course follow.

The Ten Laws of Effective Writing

1. *Nobody is born with the ability to write. Learning how to write is a process and it is one that anybody can learn given they devote appropriate time and effort to the task.*
2. *If you choose to stop at a first draft level then you will never achieve success in writing. Success in writing requires the patience and fortitude required to turn a first draft into a final draft.*
3. *Every unique writing project has a style, mood and tone appropriate for it. It is up to you to choose a style, mood and tone that will serve the greater interests of the objective of the project.*
4. *One law rules all – the more words you write the better you will become. If you simply write day in and day out you will gain skill. Nothing else can replace this. Writing is the only thing that can improve writing.*
5. *Style or voice is something acquired with time. Concern yourself with emulating other writers at first and let your unique voice emerge on its own in its proper time. It will happen. Be patient.*
6. *One of the hidden keys to good writing is to always put yourself in the reader's shoes and write words that would interest you and entertain you. As long as you entertain yourself, others will be entertained too.*
7. *Talent in writing comes from sheer volume. If you do the volume you will acquire the talent.*
8. *Word choice is a very important skill that must be sought out and acquired over time. The wider your vocabulary the better the choices you have to create sentences.*
9. *Dialogue is an art unto itself and takes many years of practice and diligence to do effectively.*
10. *How you say it is much more important than what you say. Concentrate on saying things in the most effective, interesting and entertaining way possible.*

WEEK 1
PLANNING

Before you ever write a word of a novel or a non-fiction project you should have on paper a plan. This means that you already know the scenes and what order they are in for a story and that you know each chapter you will be writing and the general content in each of the non-fiction book. If you are writing an article then you should have on paper the content of each paragraph that will make up your article. This is a necessity because a plan ensures that you have already thought through the project and worked out any problems that might come up. If you choose to work without a plan then what will happen is that you will spend a lot of time writing material that eventually has to be thrown away because it doesn't fit with the rest of the material. Planning prevents this and gives you the opportunity to make these decisions at the onset rather than wasting precious writing time doing the same process.

For a novel, planning means story development. Story development is the process by which you formulate a story from a general idea and develop it through to a series of scenes that follow a logical progression from beginning to conclusion. Story development is beyond the scope of this course. The assumption in this course is that you already have a story developed that you are ready to begin writing. If you do not have one then put this book away until you do have one. There are many techniques and variations regarding story development and it is an art unto itself.

For a non-fiction book, planning means designing the content of the chapters and the chapters themselves. This is something you can do during this course. Ideally, the best method is to first explore other books that have dealt with the subject you will be writing about. If you cannot find any then choose something that is similar. Next, you should review those books for content and chapter headings. Using those chapter headings determine what you need to cover in a chapter out of necessity, what you would like to cover out of interest and what unique way you can make your book different and better than any that have been published previously. If you cannot make an improvement on what has been previously published then drop the project and start another one. Necessity dictates that you provide a fresh perspective or new insight before you attempt writing a book about a subject that has been previously explored. The final step in planning should be a document that lists each of the chapters you intent to write as well as a brief summary of the contents of each chapter. Once you have this you are ready to begin writing.

An article is really the same thing as a book only it is condensed in form. Thus, rather than exploring a wide variety of topics you are narrowing your focus to one topic in particular. The thing you need to do is to first of all do research on your topic and make note of all the various factors that should be discussed in an article. Next you should review any books, articles or other material that has dealt with the subject matter you wish to write about. Last, you should make a plan for your article that lists each paragraph and what you will discuss within that paragraph. Once you have completed this summary then you are ready to begin writing.

WEEK 2
WRITE WHAT YOU LOVE

There is a particular reason you should choose to write something you love. That reason is called passion. If you choose to write something you are not passionate about then that lack of enthusiasm and apathy will translate over to the page and the words you write. Writing is alchemy and through it your energy and state of mind are translated to words. Therefore, a level of excitement and passion is necessary for whatever subject you choose to write about.

Before you ever begin writing you should do the following: Take a blank sheet of paper and simply begin writing down anything that interests you in life. Think about everything you can possibly imagine. Whatever it is, write it down. This project should take at least a week or two to complete and even after you are finished you should continue to add material to it as that material comes to mind. What you are doing is creating a list of things you can write about. If it is not on this list then you should probably not write about it.

There is another reason you should passionate about the subject you are writing about. That reason is called research. Whether you are writing a novel or a non-fiction book or even an article you are going to spend an inordinate amount of time researching the topic and subject matter of what you intend to write. This process can be laborious at best therefore an innate level of interest is necessary to make it palpable. If you are not interested and fascinated by the subject you are researching then your research will not be as thorough and diligent as it should have been and the result will be a manuscript that is insufficient and not worth publishing.

There is a problem however that everyone faces. That problem crops up when you are midway through the writing project. Somewhere between the beginning and the end you will be overcome with boredom about your subject even if it was interesting to you before. Mostly this is purely the result of burnout. It is a human tendency but it is also an enemy of good writing. What you must do to counteract this is do everything you possibly can to regenerate that initial level of excitement and interest that you had before beginning the project. There are many ways to do this but one way is to simply read over all your initial notes on the project when you were passionate about it. Hopefully, that will have the ability to get you back into that frame of mind.

WEEK 3
WRITING IS EXPLORATION

The reason people read is to expand their mind and their experience of life. Reading is essentially the gathering of information. If you want to find yourself bored then try reading a textbook about something you are an expert on. You will soon find yourself skimming over words and paragraphs and essentially not processing a word of what is being said. The same lesson applies when you read a fiction book and start skimming when the main character begins endlessly talking about her emotions and feelings on a subject that everyone understands. Essentially there is no new information and therefore there is no interest level in the reader. Book at their essence are about exploration. They are about opening doors to new experiences, new places, new people and new ideas. If your book has none of these characteristics then you can be sure it will be read with the brevity of a firefly light.

So what can you do as a writer to ensure that your reader stays interested and enjoys reading your book? The answer is simple. You must give the reader an experience of exploring some subject, character or location in a way that is entertaining, surprising and informative. Actually we will discuss developing the aspect of entertainment and surprise later in the course. For now lets just focus on the fact that you need to be introducing something that is new and unique in the minds of the reader.

Let's illustrate an example. Let's pretend that we are developing a murder mystery. All we know is that someone kills someone and someone must find out who the killer is and then bring them to justice. Pretty rough plot at this point. What can we do to instantly make this basic idea both interesting and entertaining to the average reader? The answer is simple. We need to find a unique background or setting or situation in which to explore the age old theme of murder and mystery. Without a unique angle the story will be forgettable and purely fodder for the worms. It is at this point that you need to engage your imagination and think about thinks that interest or intrigue you and see if you can set them into the story that you have developed up to this point. So what you do is take out your lists of interests that we made earlier in the course and see which one you can plug into the story to give it the edge and uniqueness it needs to be a winner.

Pretend that you had the following three things listed on your interest list: reincarnation, Hinduism and India and College Football. Let's see what happens when we combine these ideas with the story skeleton we currently have in place. Can you imagine the way reincarnation might figure into a murder story? There are myriad ways that the theme of reincarnation could be incorporated to the age old mystery story and each of these ways would make the tale both interesting and entertaining. The same goes for Hinduism and India. There are myriad ways that particular theme can be used to create interest in the reader and keep him hooked as you develop the same basic story he has read numerous times in the past. Though he knows what will happen he will keep reading because of the unique angle you have placed within the story that allows him to explore something he was not previously aware of before.

Hopefully, this illustrated at a basic level how you should incorporate the possibility of exploration into a story to make it both interesting and unique to the average reader. This is only one step in the process though. The next step is actually incorporating this new information into the text and scenes of the story. We will discuss methods by which you can do this later in the course. For now, simply play with story ideas you have had in the bank of your mind by combining them with particular interests you have in life. Combine them and see what comes up. It might be something worth writing about. And more importantly, it might be that certain something that many readers would love to read about.

WEEK 4
THE FIRST DRAFT

One of the first real obstacles to becoming a professional writer is both understanding what the first draft is and working within that framework to create your story.   Many have been the writer who has started on a story they were excited to tell only to never complete it because they were never able to get it the way they wanted in order to finish it.   They were aware of one important aspect of writing that every writer should always remember: the story you write in the first draft is NEVER the story you want to tell. However, it is a waypoint on the road to the realization of your vision. And it is this that most writers fail to completely understand.

Imagine for a moment that you are a painter. Let us say you are planning to pain a picture of a bridge. First you take pictures of the bridge and go visit the bridge and gather all the information you can about the bridge. Next you begin to sketch. You do this with an erasable pencil because you know that you will need to make changes as the painting shapes itself. Only after many rudimentary sketches are you finally able to actually begin the process of painting with oil which represents the final product of all the processes that took place before.

Writing is the same way. You cannot expect the first draft to be anything more than a sketch. All you are doing is simply getting things down on paper and basically trying to create some abstract semblance of the story you have in mind. ONLY when you have the first draft complete and in hand will you be able to go back to it and finally begin to work with it and shape it into the form of a novel that is both entertaining and publishable.

A first draft is written "on the cuff". You write it without thinking a great deal about what you are writing. You let your subconscious guide you and you just put words down on paper. If you don't know what is going to be said in dialogue between two characters then you simply write down whatever comes to mind. If you know you need some details inserted in a certain place then you just make them up realizing you will need to research them later. If you know you need a scene to take place at some point that is monumental and emotional but you have no idea then you just do the best you can and write whatever comes to mind.

Only after all of this is on paper and in the form of a first draft can you go back and begin to shape and mold the story into what you eventually want it to be. There are some writers who do not even use good technique the first time through a story. They are simply trying to get words on paper at this stage. They know later they will revise the scenes and extrapolate off the idea they had; they know they will do more research; they know they will fix the dialogue; they know they will write more details. The simple fact is that they know it is only a work in progress and a single step of a much longer journey. NEVER FORGET THIS. Do not try to make your first draft, final draft perfect. Let it be a first draft. Write fast and write without effort. Make up stuff as you go. Make mistakes. Blow over descriptions. Do whatever you need to do to simply get the first draft completed. There will be plenty of time later on to refine your vision and create the story you really want to tell.

The first draft is merely a first draft. As long as you remember this then you don't need to worry about anything and that frees you to simply begin putting words on paper ad infinitum until the first draft is complete. When that is complete, every writer knows, that is when the real work begins. It is then that a story creates itself.

WEEK 5
GOOD WRITING IS METHODICAL

We last discussed the first draft. Before we say anything else we need to understand that a first draft is NOT good writing. A first draft is simply getting words on paper. Therefore what we are about to discuss belongs to the stage of writing when you are trying to mold the story into its final form. It is at this stage that you begin to write in a methodical fashion and carefully consider both what you are saying and how you are saying it and even why you are saying it. All of this is important and that is why writing at this stage of the process must be well thought out and consciously methodical.

What does it mean to write methodically? Writing methodically means that you are carefully taking into consideration the effect you are trying to create in the minds of the reader and therefore you weight every word and phrase in comparison to that goal. Not only do you consider that goal but you also compare it to other novels of similar style and tone that you would consider as your potential competitors. By examining the enemy and seeing how they did what they did you can better formulate how to construct your narrative to create the effect you are striving for.

What can you do in order to write methodically? First of all you must slow down and take your time. This time you are not racing just to complete something. This time you are writing for the goal of quality and therefore it requires you test out different ways of saying something over and over in your mind until you come across the one that is right for the story you are trying to tell. Another method that can be used is to write several different versions of the scene or narrative you are trying to write and then compare and contrast, mix and max until you reach a form that is suitable to the goal you have in mind. So you either write slow knowing you are choosing the highest quality possible to create each sentence or you write for quantity simply writing as many versions of a section as you have to ensure that some of it is usable and of high quality. Do whichever is easiest for you as long as you make sure the end result is narrative of quality, literary, commercial fiction.

Another method you can use to write methodically is to actually take a similar scene or situation from a similar novel and analyze how that particular author constructed that section of text. Once you have done this you simply go back and try to do the same thing for the section you are writing. For this to work you need to choose a model that has a similar situation as compared to the one you are trying to write.

Writing is methodical and therefore one should expect that it will take time. Whereas in a first draft you can dash off a chapter per day expect than when you write methodically a particular scene may take an entire day in and of itself. Just like anything else the end result is directly related to the time and effort expended in its creation.

WEEK 6
BECOMING THE READER

It is a fact that in order to be a good writer you must be in touch with what you like and what you enjoy as a reader. Not only must you be in touch with it, but you must be conscious of it and take it into consideration as you are writing and crafting the story. The bottom line is that your goal is to write the ideal book you would love to read. As long as you do that then you will be creating an experience the writer will both enjoy and appreciate.

What does it mean in practice to become the reader? Essentially it involves the process of continually asking yourself questions through all phases of the novel process. At each stage you should be asking yourself the following question:

1) What would I like to happen here or what would I find the most appealing, interesting or entertaining?
2) What could take place that would drag me deeper into the story?
3) What surprise could take place that I would find highly entertaining?
4) What could this character do or say to make me highly attracted to them or highly repulsed by them?
5) What fantasy fulfillment could this story provide for me and how would it take place?

Those are the basic questions you need to ask yourself at every stage in the novel process. These questions are especially important in regards to story development. Then once you have the first draft down you go back and evaluate whether the scene provides the feeling you are looking for as written or do you need to revise it? By constantly writing and evaluating and refining you will eventually get to the point that the text will meet your expectations and when you reach that point you know that the novel is working.

WEEK 7
THEME

I have my own personal beliefs about stories. My beliefs go back to the foundation of literature and story telling. Stories were originally designed to do one thing primarily. Yes, they were meant to entertain but their primary function was to TEACH. Stories were designed to teach us something about life, something that we can learn through the story and thus save us the frustration of gaining the knowledge through the process of life itself. What the story teaches is its theme. And it is theme that is the ultimate foundation of any story.

How does one come up with a theme? Often, it is not by figuring out the theme first. More so, it is usually a case of having a particular story in mind and then as you begin to think about it you determine what it is that you are trying to say or trying to teach to the reader. It is not an alien though to imagine that our subconscious has in mind a particular lesson for us and then cloaks that lesson in the images and actions of a story. It is up to our conscious mind to determine exactly what that hidden message is and then once we know it is our job to clarify it and see that all the patterns and structures of the story go toward making this message clear and apparent.

All of this goes back to the original intent to our need to tell stories. And that intent is to make sense of life with all of its vicissitudes and random happenings. We need life to make sense because humans always seek a pattern in everything. It is why we watch the stars, it is why we look at history and it is why we tell stories. Humans seek to impose a pattern on existence so that it makes sense and thus there is understanding about what exactly is taking place. Stories are the oldest and the most prevalent form that we use in making sense of life. A theme is essentially something that says this is the lesson or this is the meaning behind the events. This is why things happened. This is the lesson. It is what we are looking for more than anything when we read a story. Yes, entertainment is important but without theme it is simple banal entertainment.

We all come into this world with certain "themes" that are ours alone. There is some theme that repeats itself in your life or some question you have always sought the answers for. Whatever this is, it is a reflection of your need to tell stories. Examine the deeper questions you have in your own life and then you will find the deeper themes of your own writing. Yes, it is possible to write other types of stories but these will always lack the same fire and enthusiasm that those which drive our existence seek to answer. Storytelling is an answer we make up to the questions that bother us so. There is a question we seek in our lives more than anything. A story is the story we make up to answer that question and whatever that meaning is, is the theme of our story.

WEEK 8
EXCITEMENT

There is some form of magic at work that translates the excitement we feel about a story or subject through our fingers, into the words and onto the page and into the readers mind. Whatever level of excitement we feel is somehow transmitted to the reader and this is something that cannot be explained. Thus, above all choose stories and subjects that excite you or that you are passionate about because you cannot hide your lack of interest behind words.

Life is also too short to spend time learning and reading and writing about subjects that do not interest us. Why not find something that sets your imagination on fire and that you feel passionate about? One of the practices that I do when I am looking for a subject to write about is to make a list of all the things that excite or intrigue me regardless of whether they are ideas, people, concepts, beliefs, situations, events or whatever. Once I have this list complete then I go back through it and see if there is a story to tell behind any of these words. Invariably I find one with potential and from there the rest of the story grows.

All of this also applies to writing scenes or chapters. Basically it is a process of finding something about that chapter or that scene that excites you and makes you more interested in what is happening. Whatever that is you need to accentuate it and allow it to provide the spark within the section you are writing. We all have experienced reading passages which were nothing but blasé words on paper and as a result we do nothing more than skim hoping to get to the end as soon as possible. We can avoid writing such passages by finding a spark of excitement in each sequence, scene or chapter. Whatever that spark is focus on it and expand it and entrance the reader the same way that you yourself are entranced.

WEEK 9
WRITER'S BLOCK

Writer's Block is something that happens to everyone every now and then. It is as if the muse has stopped speaking to you and you are on your own. It is a bad time in the life of every writer. However, as much as it is maligned it is not all a bad thing. Often the down time in writer's block is a way for your subconscious to cleanse your mind of old ideas and begin the process of birthing new ones. Usually after a spout of writer's block is over you will be able to return to writing fresh in both energy and in terms of story ideas.

Let's talk about some of the ways you can get through writers block and begin writing once again. There are two approaches to defeating writer's block and they are complete opposites. What works for some will not work for others and vice-versa.

Method #1 involves sitting down at your computer or writing table and putting hands to the keyboard or pen to paper and begin writing anything and everything that comes to mind. This is called free association. Whatever you do, don't judge the process or pause to reflect on what you are thinking and what is being written. Simply write whatever comes to mind. If you are thinking, "I have nothing in mind" then write exactly that! After doing this for a period of time eventually you will come to a place where once again a story or a scene begins to take shape. That should be all the confidence you need to begin writing regularly once again.

Method #2 involves taking an existing work that you admire and that inspires you and to either begin copying it exactly as it is or taking a different character and placing him in a similar scene or starting a story in a similar manner. Often this will spur your imagination on toward your own writing endeavors and allow you to begin writing once again. This is the method that works best for me. In fact I often use this method when I am trying to capture a certain mood in a novel and I know of another author has done that successfully. I simply take the book in which the mood is captured and begin copying it until I get to the point that my own ideas begin to take shape. Try it. You will be surprised how successful this method can be.

There is another form of writer's block that we need to talk about. This is the all the more dreaded version. This is the writer's block you have when inspiration has completely left you and been replaced by a mild short of depression and lack of enthusiasm for anything including life itself. This is a serious problem and there is really not much you can do about it except to wait until it passes. You will know this problem has struck when the ideas and stories that usually excite you do nothing to stimulate you or arouse your imagination. Usually, what is taking place is that you are going through a growth period in your soul and therefore you must wait until your subconscious has processed things and is ready to move on with life. There is nothing you can do to rush the process. Fortunately, most writers only experience this problem a handful of times during their entire lifetime. When it happens to you just grin and bear it and know that in time it too will pass.

WEEK 10
MAKING WRITING A HABIT – 10 PAGES A DAY

To approach writing in a professional manner and to expect to make a living at it you must give it the same amount of effort that you would give any other traditional job. To do less and expect results is simply not realistic. The sooner you realize this the sooner you will be on your way to making real progress toward the goal of getting published. Legion are the number of writers who profess to be such but yet spend very little time actually writing on any given day. This simply will not work. You must writer every day or at the least five days a week for a set number of hours or set amount of volume. It is usually best to judge by volume of output since one can spend innumerable hours staring at the computer screen or doing something else while you are waiting for the muse to inspire you.

I would challenge you to make your goal at least 10 pages a day. However, I will say up front that a set number of pages a day has always confused me. I mean after all there are various sizes of pages that makes such a goal hard to quantify. A much better and more realistic goal is to decide on a word count for the average page and then proceed from there. A good word total for an average page is 200 words. Thus a goal of 10 pages a day is actually 10,000 words. Work from the word total as opposed to the page count. Do the same thing when scheduling the writing for your novel. Shoot for a specific word count on a daily basis and you will surely make the progress that you intend to make toward completing the book.

WEEK 11
POINT OF VIEW

One of the first major decisions you will make when deciding to write a story is what point of view to use. Most beginners choose to write in First Person because it is more natural and simply easier to write than third person. The choice of point of view should depend on the story you are telling. Certain stories will lend themselves to one style or the other. Therefore the thing to do is think about the story and which point of view will make the most effective presentation in the mind of the reader.

There are three basic points of view that you can write from. They are as follows:

1) First Person – This is when you write the story as if you are the person the action is happening to or that it had happened to. An example of this point of view would be the following: *"I didn't know exactly what to think of the situation I got myself into. All I knew was that there would be trouble but at that time I didn't know exactly how bad it would get. Only later did I find that the simple word trouble was an understatement."*

2) Second Person – Second person is very seldom used. In fact they only style of writing you will find it in is in the "choose your own adventure" books that are so popular with children. An example of this style of writing follows: *"You wake up earlier than normal with a distinct feeling that something is not right. Without knowing why you get out of bed and put on your clothes and walk outside the castle. It is there that you discover the feeling for your disquiet. All of the horses lay dead with no apparent culprit to be found. What will you do now?"*

3) Third Person – This point of view is often called Omniscient. This is because when writing in this style it is taken for granted that the narrator can go inside the heads of the characters and also see events in the past and the future. This is the point of view that is most popular in fiction writing. Some writers

will limit the omniscience of the narrator to knowledge of just the protagonist. This is called "Limited Omniscience". An example of third person follows: *"The rains were worse than they had been in a 100 years. It had flowed into the valleys and inundated the plains creating large standing pools of water that were in some place deep enough to drown someone. So it was that on the day of July 4th, Eugene Allister found himself helping a family he barely knew drag their model-T from the confines of a particularly deep puddle. Little did he know how this event would be the beginning of what would become the ending of his life."*

Choosing a point of view to write in is often a matter of weighing the needs of the reader. You need to take the time to put yourself in the shoes of the reader and try to imagine experiencing the story you want to tell from that viewpoint. What you will find is that some stories will more naturally flow in first person while others require that they be told in third person to convey the feeling you would like to convey. Obviously if the thoughts and feelings of multiple characters are integral to the story then writing in third person is probably the right choice. However, if the particular character and uniqueness of the narrator is the primary draw of the story then the best choice is most likely first person. A good writer should be comfortable writing from any of these points of views and learn to choose between them in the same way a painter will choose a certain brush to create a certain effect in the painting he is in the process of completing.

WEEK 12
FINDING THE MUSE

Those who are not writers will have a hard time understanding the concept of "the muse". However for a writer it becomes an idea that takes on a reality of its own. It is derived from the myth in ancient times which said each writer or poet was inspired by god through a divine spirit or "muse". Thus gifted writers were often said to be "possessed by the muse". The ideology has filtered down to today where we often hear writers of every style and genre refer to the muse as if it were a physical entity.

Think of the muse as being the wellspring for your ideas and the passion and excitement that comes with a new idea. Without the muse you are left idealess and without inspiration and it is for this reason that every writer curses the day when the muse is no longer with them. Unfortunately, like writers block, this is something that happens from time to time. What you need to understand is that it just takes some time and patience to get past it before the muse will once again inspire you to greatness.

Many writers have formulated certain methods that best inspires them and enhances their creativity. For some this is done with music. For others it is done by turning off all the lights and writing in the dark. For others it is reading something inspirational like the bible before you write. Or perhaps it entails writing at a certain time at night or early in the morning. The methods of various and diverse but as you begin to write with more and more regularity you will find that certain things, atmospheres or surroundings are more conducive to your creativity than others. The key is to find out what the particular combination is that works best for you and then to repeat that each and every time you write. By creating a familiar atmosphere you will inspire yourself to duplicate the best efforts you have enjoyed in the past.

Experiment with various surroundings and stimuli when you write. Try writing while drinking coffee. Try writing in the dark. Try writing late at night or early in the morning. Try writing with earphones on listening to music. Try writing after reading something you find inspirational. Try writing after copying the words of a famous author you enjoy. Try anything! The key is that you find something that inspires you and allows you to find the muse that feeds you the words and stories which are uniquely your own.

WEEK 13
WRITING FROM A MODEL

There is one thing that every beginning writer must do in order to learn the craft. That one thing is to write from a model. It means that you don't go off on your own but instead use a successful novel as your guide in constructing your own fiction. It is a necessity for leaning the craft at the highest level.

What does it mean to write from a model? First let's look at the way in which you would choose an appropriate model. Then we will look at the ways to utilize that model in your own writing. First of all decide what genre the story is you plan to write. Once you have done this go through and examine as many possible writers as possible of that type of fiction. After you have reviewed them you should be able to pinpoint a fair number that are similar to what you have in mind. The next step is to buy those novels and read them before you begin your own. This way you will be able to establish how and in what manner yours is different than the preceding novels. Once this is completed then you are ready to move on to the next step of modeling.

Modeling requires that you assimilate the spirit of the novel you are copying. This applies to tone and style and word choice mainly. Ideally when you are modeling you should be able to copy these characteristics very easily. If you cannot at first then give it time because eventually it will take place.

Step #1 in modeling is to take the prototype novel and plot it out chapter by chapter. What you are looking for is the pattern by which subplots and plots are laid out in the final manuscript. You should seek to use a similar pattern. This should be to the point that if a model book has subplot D in Chapter 5 then yours should have the same. So the first step of modeling is the big picture – Chapter construction and layout.

Step #2 is the chapter itself. This is the point when you dissect an individual chapter and use it to manufacture your own chapter. The way to do this is to pay attention to what the author has used to build the scene and then for you to use the same components in building your own scene. Thus if an author has a scene with two characters and a horrendous event you should strive to have the same.

Modeling only becomes clear on repetition. The more you do it the more you will understand exactly what it is that you are doing. For that reason the best thing to do is simply choose a book you admire and dive in by modeling it with your own fictional world.

WEEK 14
RESEARCH

Research is certainly a subject that could have an entire book devoted to it. Good research often makes the difference between a very good novel and one that is only passable. Good research is the key to really dragging the reader into your fictional world and making the experience seem lifelike and realistic.

Research does not always have to be done upfront. Many writers will write from their head so to speak only to come back later and add the researched details and finer points that were missed in the first draft. There is no real reason not to do it this way other than the fact that editing a first draft is always a bit more detail oriented than simply adding those details in on the first draft.

Researching up front is not only an easier way to do things but it is also a good source for story material. Often a writer will use research of a particular topic in the objective of creating the story. The more detailed and specific your research the more of the same will be your story. The key is to know where to expend your energy and what exactly it is you are looking for.

One way to look at research is as a search to find things that interests you. What you are hoping to find is some material that you find fascinating and then you can use that material and as a result transfer that fascination you feel to the fictional world you are creating in your book. If you find that things do not fascinate you then you are probably best served by choosing a different subject to write about. Life is too short to write books you wouldn't even want to read yourself. You should always be writing something that you would love to read. In this way you ensure at least 1 fan on the completion of your novel.

WEEK 15
A STORY IS ABOUT "SOMEBODY"

Many who desire to tell a story find it natural to think in terms of events or situation, I myself write in this manner. However, often it is these same types of people who have a difficult time creating a story around an individual person. And any story must be about a central character or we move from telling a story to reporting an event. For it is the human character at the central of a story that gives us the ability to move inside and inhabit the words on a page.

There are those of you who will protest and point out stories about various kinds of animals, aliens or even other abstract constructs such as pure consciousness beings or the force of nature. Do these follow the same rule? Yes they do. The reason they still fall within the realm of being about a human is because the writer has taken an abstract non-human entity and humanized it by giving it the typical human motivations, goals, fears and desires. Thus as a reader we think we are reading about something else when in fact we are simply reading another human-centered story incognito.

To discuss why stories require this particular constraint would require an in depth discussion on biology, consciousness and human development. Something we don't have time or knowledge necessary to get into. Thus, the best thing to do is just accept it at face value and immediately put into the waste basket all those stories describing things or events without an identifiable protagonist or create such protagonist and begin the same story anew from a different perspective.

Let's go through a process of making a story subjective and human-centric that in its original form is more abstract and non-character based. For example, suppose we want to do a story about an earthquake that devastates the western portion of the United States. We could start the story off by describing the situation and then proceed to the event by only using cursory characterizations of the human beings within the story. It is entirely possible that the entire event could be written in this way. The question is this: Would we as readers find it compelling as a "story"? The answer is, no, we would not. So what would we need to do in order to create a compelling story for a reader? Simple, we must create a human protagonist – someone whom we can identify with – and give them goals, fears and situations that we ourselves can relate to and understand. When we do this then we can immediately see how it is the human "quantity" on an individual level that turns something into "story". Anything without this is mere reportage and summary which we can find in newspapers and history books but not on the best selling fiction list.

Examine your story ideas and determine if any of them suffer from this problem. If they do begin to re-imagine them in the context of a human entity with fears, hopes and desires that the reader can relate and respond to.

WEEK 16
A STORY INVOLVES "ACTION"

Last week we discussed the problem with stories without human protagonist. This week we will focus on the other common problem with story development: lack of action or movement.

Let us begin by defining a story as being a description of change and causal effects. Since change requires time then we naturally fall into the classic three act structure or subdivisions of beginning, middle and end. ALL stories will fall into these criteria. The reason they do so is due to the fact that everything that we experience is causally related to something else and takes place within a relational world.

I would like to quote at length a portion of the book "Three Roads to Quantum Gravity" by Lee Smolin. You are probably wondering how a book on quantum gravity can possibly relate to writing and story development. A very good question which will be answered once you read the following excerpt from Chapter Four: The Universe is Made of Processes not Things.

"Imagine you are trying to explain to someone why you are so enamored of your new girlfriend or boyfriend and someone quite sensibly asks you to describe them. Why do our efforts on such occasions seem so inadequate? Your intuition tells you that there is something essential about this person, but it is very hard to put into words. You describe what they do for a living, what they like to do for fun, what they look like, how they act, but somehow this does not seem to convey what they are really like.

There is a simple solution to this quandary: tell a story. If we narrate the story of our new friend's life, where and how they grew up, who their parents are and how they raised them, where they studied, what happened in their past relationships, we communicate more of what is important about them than if we attempt to describe how they are now.

The question is this: What is it about a person that makes it hard to describe without telling a story? The answer is we are not dealing with a thing, like a rock or can opener. These are objects which more or less remain the same from decade to decade. They can be described, for most purposes, as static objects, each with some collection of unchanging properties. But when we are dealing with a person or other things such as a culture or a history or a movement, we are dealing with a process that cannot be comprehended as a static object, independently of its history. How it is now is incomprehensible without knowing how it came to be.

Just what is it about a story that tells us so much? What extra information are we conveying when we tell a story? When we tell a story we narrate a series of events or episodes in something "life". These tell us something about the person because we believe, from having heard and understood many such stories, that what happens to a person as they grow up has an effect on who they are. We also believe that a persons character is best revealed in how they react to situation, both propitious and adverse and in what they have sought to do or become.

However, it is not the events themselves that carry information in a narration. A mere list of events is very boring and not a story. This is perhaps what Andy Warhol was trying to convey in his movies of haircuts or of a day in the life of the Empire State Building. What makes a story a story are the CONNECTIONS between events. These may be explicit, but they often do not need to be, because we fill them in almost unconsciously. We can do that because we all believe that events in the past are to some extent the cause of events in the future. We can debate to what extant a person is shaped by what happens to them, but we do not need to be devout determinists to have a practical and almost instinctual understanding of the important of causality. It is this understanding of causality that makes stories useful. Who did what to whom, and when and why is interesting because of what we know about the consequences of events.

Imagine what the world would be like without causality. Suppose that the history of the world were no more than random sets of events with no causal connections between them. Thing would just happen; nothing would remain in place. Can you imagine what that world would be like? It is causality that gives our world its structure (and the same goes for stories). And it is because of the overwhelming importance of causal relationships in shaping our world that stories are much more informative than descriptions.

So it seems that there are two different kinds of entities in the world. There are objects like rocks and can openers that simple ARE, that may be completely explained by their properties. And there are things that can only be comprehended as processes that can only be explained by telling stories. For things of the second kind, a simple description never suffices. A story is the only adequate description of them because entities like people and cultures are not really things; they are processes unfolding in time.

We humans seem to be fascinated by our ability to hold back change for long periods of time. This may be why painting and sculpture are so fascinating and so valuable, for they offer the illusion that time can be stopped. But time cannot be stopped. A marble sculpture may look the same from day to day, but it is not: each day the surface becomes a little different as the marble interacts with the air. All the skill of an artist cannot turn a process into a thing, for there are no things, only processes that appear to change slowly for our human timescales. Even objects that seem not to change, like rocks and can openers, have stories. It is just that the timescale over which they change is significantly longer to appear unchanging to our human scale of time. Geologist and cultural historians are very interested in narrating the stories of rocks and can openers.

So there are not really only two categories of things in the world: objects and processes. There are only relatively fast processes and relatively slow processes. And whether it is a short story or long story, the only kind of explanation of a process that is adequate is to tell a story.

From this point of view, the universe consists of a large number of EVENTS. An event may be thought of as the smallest unit of change. But do not think of an event as a change happening to an otherwise static object. It is just a change, no more than that.

The universe of events is a RELATIONAL UNIVERSE. That is, all its properties are described in terms of the relationships between the events. The most important relationship that two events can have is causality. This is the same notion of causality that we found essential to make sense of stories.

Such a universe has TIME built into it from the beginning. Time and change are not optional, for the universe is a story and it is comprised of processes. In such a world, time and causality are synonymous. There is no meaning to the past of an event except the set of events that caused it. And there is no meaning to the future of an event except the set of events it will influence.

Most, if not all beginning writers make the same mistake time and time again. The mistake is in using summaries instead of writing scenes. This is probably the number one mistake for most beginning writers. Rather than write scenes they write summaries and as a result an exciting story becomes nothing but a boring report.

In order to better understand the difference lets give an example of what we are talking about.

SUMMARY:

> *The rain was hard and unforgiving. She could barely see through the windshield to the road ahead. She only hopped that she was staying on her side or bad weather would be the least of her concerns. Thoughts of Angel and everything that happened regarding him swam through her mind. She couldn't help but feel she had made a mistake by leaving.*

SCENE :

> *Lightning crashed across the sky and rain peppered the windshield as she frantically drove through the storm. Her knuckles were white from clutching the steering wheel so had.*
>
> *"Damn this weather!" she said aloud to no one in particular.*
>
> *She quickly rummaged through the glove box to get her cigarettes. She lit one as she swerved to get back on the road.*
>
> *"Angel where are you now?" she thought. She couldn't keep her mind clear of everything that happened between them.*

Okay that is probably not the best example but it is the best I could come up with at the moment. Essentially the difference is that in a scene you actually describe the events as IF they are happening whereas in a summary you are simply giving a report of things that happened. A scene is involving and engages the reader whereas a report is distant and objective. As a writer job numero uno is to engage the reader. Hence you must write scenes rather than reports.

However, there are times when a summary is more appropriate. Anything description of a long length of time is one example. Another is when you are simply giving background and history to a story. Both of these examples would be bogged down by writing in scene format. Thus summary is the tool of choice.

To better understand the differences between the two try writing a section of your story in both summary format and scene format. When you finish, read the two and see which one you like better.

WEEK 18
TRANSITIONS

Transitions are another structural device that can make the difference between publishable and non-publishable fiction. A transition is the doorway leading from one scene to the next. A good transition is smooth and appropriate while an awkward transition or the lack of one makes the story awkward and hard to read.

Though we are talking about transitions more often than not it is the paragraph before the transition that determines its effectiveness. The effect you are striving for is a story that moves from one scene to the next effortlessly and without notice. You do this by giving the reader clues and hints that a transition is about to take place, thus when it comes it is not even noticed. How do you do this? Look at the following examples:

Transition by Dialogue

He slammed the door shut to the office. Margaret cringed. "Tomorrow I expect the report to be finished! Do you understand?" With that he stormed out of the office leaving her to piece together something before he returned. "God there is no way I can do this." She thought to herself as she turned on the computer and began typing. It was going to be a long, long night.

She arrived at work thirty minutes earlier so she would have time to put the finishing touches on the disaster of a report she finished at 3:00 AM.

(Notice, how the preceeding paragraph gives a "closing" of sorts and gives the reader a clue that the next paragraph will pick up somewhere in the future?)

Here is a more professional example by Somerset Maugham's The Colonel's Lady:

"I expect it'll be very dull, but they're making a point of it. And the day after, the American Publisher who's taken my book is giving a cocktail party at Claridge's. I'd like you to come to that if you wouldn't mind."

"Sounds like a crashing bore, but if you really want me to come I'll come."

"It would be sweet of you."

George Peregrine was dazed at the cocktail party....

Transition by Narration

Margaret knew who it was before she looked up from the way he slammed the door. It was her boss again. He had dropped in just to remind her that he needed the report from her first thing in the morning. Of course he added an insult or two along with the request. She quickly opened the document and started working on it as soon as he had left. It was going to be a very long night.

Here is another example of the same technique from the story Things by D.H. Lawrence:

However, New York was not all America. There was the great clan West. So the Melville's went West, with Peter, but without the things. They tried living a simple life, in the mountains. But doing their own chores became almost a nightmare....A Millionaire friend came to the rescue, offering them a cottage on the California coast...with joy the idealist moved a little further West.

Let's see the change needed in a typical transition by illustration. Following you will find a student submitted story section:

Frank Smith ordered his secretary to get him the reservation on the eleven o'clock plane for Washington and to wire Senator Davis he was coming. He wondered what the Senator wanted, as he rode in the taxi from his office to his apartment. After packing an overnight bag, he took a taxi to the airport. Upon arrival at the Washington airport, he took a taxi

*to the Senate Office Building. The Senator's secretary told him
the Senator was waiting for him and to go right in.*

*"I appreciate you coming at once," the Senator said as
they shook hands.*

A more effective transition for this story can be illustrated using
dialogue:

*Frank Smith pushed down the intercom button on his
desk. "Miss Jones, get me a reservation on the eleven o'clock
plane for Washington, and wire Senator Davis I'll be in his
office by one o'clock."*
*"I appreciate you coming at once," Senator Davis said
as Frank entered the Senator's office.*

The transition can be made even shorter by using narrative:

*Frank Smith asked his secretary to get him a plane
reservation for Washington and to wire Senator Davis that he
would be there by one o'clock.*
*"I appreciate you coming at once," Senator Davis said
as Frank entered the office.*

WEEK 19
SHOW DON'T TELL

When you first begin writing you will have a tendency to simply write as if you are telling someone a story. One would think this is the correct manner to in fact write a story. But it is not. In fact, the correct way to write a story is to write it as if it is happening to the person you are telling it to. This is a key difference that can be illustrated by describing how to "show" and how to "tell".

When we "tell" something then we are giving the reader a description of an event, person or place by using words that are in essence judgments. In a sense we insert ourselves in between the event and the interpretation of the event. For example, I might see an old man on the street in tattered clothes and decide to call him a "derelict". You, on the other hand might see the same old man and decide to call him a "victim of the system". This is simply two different ways of interpreting the same visual data – a man with old clothes, dirty and unshaven. Therefore when we "tell" something we are in essence removing the reader from participation in the scene. This is obviously what we don't want to do.

"Showing", as the antithesis of "telling" involves giving the reader all of the data which he needs in order to draw his own conclusions. Obviously this entails that we give good and thorough descriptions of everything – which by itself is a predicate to good story telling. Let's give an example to make clear what we are talking about. If we were to "show" rather than tell, the description of the old man above might read like this:

> *"The old man's dingy brown suit was tattered at the sleeves and worn at the elbows. It was dirty and the original coloring was hidden behind layers and layers of stains of a variety of things. His face was unshaved and his mouth bore the perpetual sneer of somebody who has a complete distaste for whatever it is he is experiencing".*

Not the greatest but you hopefully get the idea. The key is that you create a description of the character or scene and let the reader draw their own conclusions as to its meaning. When you do this you invite the reader to participate in the story which heightens meaning and interest.

WEEK 20
INTEGRATING INFORMATION AND EXPLORATION INTO THE STORY

We often think we read fiction only for entertainment. This is really not the truth. The fact is we read to learn just and to experience and it is these things that we often come to describe as "entertainment". Therefore, the entertainment we seek brings us new experiences and knowledge and it this that the writer should focus on, knowing that the entertainment will come as a result.

We want to be specific about what it is we are calling "information" and "exploration". Information could be better defined by adding the word "new" in front of it. This is because when we learn something we already know then we are likely to have a minimum level of interest. However when we read something new then our interest is heightened and we will seek to learn more as long as the subject is interesting to us. Obviously what interests us is a difficult thing to judge, which is why as writers we should write what we are interested in with the knowledge that more than likely there is someone else interested in the same thing.

So we have defined "information" as being both new and interesting to us. We can further define information according to the genre of the book which we are writing. For example, romance readers seek to learn about love and the new ways it can be experienced; action/adventure seek to learn about new places and situations which test the strength and resolve of the hero to overcome forces set to destroy him; military readers seek information on the experience of battle and war and how courage and strength can bring about victory; fantasy and science fiction readers seek to experience new worlds and alien civilizations, cultures and creations, etc. Therefore we can look to the genre we right to determine exactly what new information we are being asked to provide and thus we can ensure that the book we are writing as unique information of this quality.

Therefore knowing what it is we need to add to a story, it is now only a matter of adding it. This is where you have to be careful that you not merely add words for the sake of exposition. Somehow it should be made relevant to the story. For example, if I am doing a novel on Antarctica and I have a great deal of interesting stuff that I want to add then I must do it in such a way that it is relevant to the story. This might take place in a conversation between scientists or it might take place at a conference or whatever else. The key is it must take place and be communicated in a meaningful way within the story as opposed to merely being added on exposition with no story purpose.

WEEK 21
STYLE AND WORD CHOICE

Sometimes it is helpful to think of words as having a particular personality or color or flavor. And if you think about this they really do! For example let's consider a subject and then look at various words we could use to describe this subject. We will use the scene of a person rising to meet the day on some particular morning. The thing we want to describe is the "morning" and how it is perceived by our protagonist. Words we could use follow:

1. Brilliant – We could use this word and immediately we get a positive, optimistic and happy feeling about our protagonist and the story.
2. Somber – This immediately puts a downspin on the story and makes us think of a more depressing character and situation.
3. Dreary – Again this is colored similar to the above word.
4. Foggy – This makes us have a feeling of uncertainty and vagueness about things.

You should get the idea by now. The words you use actually create the mood and the reader's perception and expectations of the story. This is very important to understand. If you have read a story that struck you as incongruent then it is probably because of the wrong words telling the wrong story. If you read any great writer you will see that they hit upon the same themes over and over and create the same type of mood throughout their story except when they desire to create a different mood. The way they do this is through word choice. The difference between the right word and the wrong word is legion.

Go back and pick up a book by an author famed for a certain type of book. Horror writers are the easiest to pick out. Try an Anne Rice book or a Stephen King or an Edgar Allen Poe. Pick out a passage at random and look for words that build a certain mood. I will do this now for illustration.

Here is an excerpt from Anne Rice's "Queen of the Damned":

*"Here Maharet had once guided her through total
DARKNESS, down into the water and along a path of STONES.
Mael had joined them. Maharet had poured wine for Jesse and
they had sung a song Jesse could never recall afterwards,
though now she would find herself humming this EERIE melody
with inexplicable accuracy, then stop, aware of it, unable to
find the proper note again."*

Notice how these words are all of a similar quality and how
even the names of the characters contribute to the mood they
create. Anne Rice, being a master of the craft, does this not
only with the words and names but even with the scene itself
which creates the same haunting quality as the words.

I will let you do the same thing with authors of your own
choosing to see if you can see the same principle illustrated. If
they are a writer of any worth you will certainly find the same
consistency between words, names and scenes which overall
create the specific mood of the entire work.

WEEK 22
PREWRITING THE SCENE

When you find yourself having difficulty with a particular scene or section of your book you should try "prewriting" it to clarify your thoughts and the direction you want the scene to take. Prewriting is essentially the same thing as a "treatment" in screenwriting. It is writing about what happens without actually making it into a novelistic form. You are just describing what happens and what events occur in the story along with any moods or information you want the reader to get from that particular section. Later on, you will actually take this and write the actual novel from these sections. Obviously saying you want to plant information on the characters background in the civil war is much different than actually doing it. However, where prewriting helps is in the event you find yourself stuck and unable to move forward because of an inability to describe the scene or section like you would like. Prewriting frees you to just note down the intent and move on to completion of the story. Later, after you have written subsequent sections you will often find you are clearer about a previous section.

You are probably wondering how prewriting is different than an outline. The key is that prewriting is closer to the actual form the novel will take. With an outline you simply note events and actions whereas with prewriting you also put down specific moods and other literary techniques as well. Some find it helpful and others do not. The key is to use it if it works for you and if you are stuck you might want to try it even if you don't think this technique is for you.

WEEK 23
SCENE PURPOSE

Every scene that is in your book must serve a purpose. To understand why, you need only take a moment to think about why you are telling a story. You are telling a story to create a feeling or an experience for the reader. The words, events and descriptions are the tools you use to achieve this. And all of these should be brought together in harmony to guide, lead and even snooker the reader into the feeling you are attempting to impart to him. Any scene that does not contribute to this will water down your focus and in effect give you much less of a chance in reaching your objective.

Let us refine this even further. We say that a scene must have a purpose but what are these viable purposes? This is a simpler question that it might seem. One could say that the objective of a scene is to give background on the characters abused childhood, or to tell of the history of the necklace or to show the machinations going on beyond the comprehension of the character, etc, etc. You can go on forever with these types of things. However, it is much more concise and understandable if we can just agree on the fact that what we are attempting to do is change a VALUE in the mind of the reader. So in essence you begin with the end in mind and then work backward to ensure your seen fulfills the objective.

Let's go through an example to illustrate this principle. We will use the classic movie, "Star Wars" as the model. Even though it is a movie the same principles also apply to novels because they are both forms of storytelling. We will use the first three scenes for illustration.

1. Scene 1 – The story opens with Leia being pursued by Imperial guards and ends with her communicating something to the droid R2-D2 after which the droid leaves on an escape pod and the princess is captured.
    a. OBJECTIVE – When George Lucas was writing this his thought about the opening scene was probably the idea of setting up the conflict of the

story as soon as possible. Because it is a conflict we always want the audience or the reader to sympathize with one party at the expense of the other. Thus, Lucas paints the Princess in the sympathetic plight of being pursued and then uses his other resources to add to this effect. (She wears white, she is a human while those pursuing her wear masks for the most part, etc.) So the value that Lucas sought to create in this scene was SYMPATHY. He could have done this in many numerous ways and they might have worked just as well. In a sense it is truly the ends that matter as opposed to the means. As long as you create the response you want from your reader then you have accomplished your goal.

2. Scene 2 – We are now in a desert wasteland and soon introduced to the protagonist of the story Luke Skywalker. The scene paints the picture of his longing for adventure and more from life than that which he has now.

    a. All great masters of fiction whether in screen or narrative form, know that alternating between high emotion and low emotion creates a greater effect than simply maintaining high emotion throughout. Therefore Lucas probably had as an objective for this scene to be a more prosaic and reflective scene to create contemplation in the audience. But he also needed to plant a seed for the story to come and he did this by Luke's longings and yearning. The other objective of this scene is to create a question in the mind of the audience as to how this scene is connected to the prior one. Because we natural seek completion this creates a need to see the question answered and thus captures the attention of the audience.

WEEK 24
The Opening Scene

There is nothing more critical in a dramatic work than the opening moments. It is during this time that your audience forms conceptions and opinions about your story and makes the decision to devote more of their time to it or not. If you lose the audience here then regaining them is near impossible. Thus, it is important to have an opening scene that makes the audience want to know more. Regardless of how else you say it, the fact is that people stay with something because they want to know more. This week will be devoted to understanding how and why that occurs and what steps you can take to make sure that you opening scene leaves them begging for more.

One principle that you will find throughout this course is "self-knowledge". Self-knowledge means that by understanding yourself you can figure out what you need to do in any given situation. Therefore, the first question to ask is what is it that makes you want to continue watching a movie or reading a book? What is it that hooks you into the story? The answers will certainly vary but most of them will fall into one of the following categories:

1. A *unique and intriguing character*, setting or situation which you want to learn more about.
2. A *"mystery" or question posed* at the opening that you seek to resolve by watching or reading more.
3. A general *"feeling"* that the opening generates for you that you would like to experience further. (This is often the case with comedies. The hook is the funny scene at the beginning and because of it you want to see more funny scenes.)
4. An *indignity or injustice perpetrated* on someone that you would like to see avenged.
5. An extremely *terrible loss incurred* by someone or some place that you would like to see recovered.
6. A *unique viewpoint* that captivates you.

Looking over these typical responses it is easy to see a pattern. The pattern is the need for completion. Because we naturally seek completion in our lives, anything that leaves something unresolved has the potential to provide a story hook. However, as you might guess some hooks are much stronger than others. The strongest hook makes a personal connection with something in the viewer or reader.

Thus, for a writer (whether of screenplays or novels) the key thing to determine is whether or not you have a hook in your opening sufficient enough to snag the average reader or movie-goer. If you do not then you have not done your job sufficiently and need to scrap the old scene and try something new. Regardless of whether or not the rest is any good, without a solid opening it will never be given a chance by the average person.

The best thing to do is to use the above list as a guideline (which is certainly not extensive) in determining appropriate hooks. If you try to add more avoid thinking of them from the perspective as a writer and instead focus on your own responses from the perspective of a reader or a viewer. And above all be sure you have an opening that snags your audience and won't let go until your story reaches its conclusion.

WEEK 25
Drama and Narrative

There are really only two methods of writing a book and of course there is also the combination of these two methods. There is drama or scene in which the action plays out before the readers eyes as if it were taking place while they are present. This is the method from which most drama derives. The other method is narrative and it is this method that seeks to compress time and give a rendition of events in which only the important things are noted. Important, meaning things which somehow influence or reflect upon the story taking place.

Most stories will use a combination of these two methods of writing. However, if one reviews any amount of classical literature it becomes apparent that the narrative story was far more popular. As time has passed drama or scenes have become the far more common alternative with stories using a combination of the two still the most popular. Television is not separated from this phenomenon where recently we have scene the likes of "24" which seeks to tell the events of an entire day over a course of a years worth of shows. This was anticipated by the popularity of the twenty-four hour novel which reached its peak many years ago. Thus, we can see how all dramatic forms tend to follow a similar pattern and how techniques go in and out of fashion as time goes on.

For the beginning novelist the important thing is to understand both story telling devices and to be able to write in either form as the situation is called for. Sometimes one will find a scenic treatment to be superior while at other times narrative will be the far better alternative. The characteristics of each form are important to understand when determining which is appropriate for a particular portion of a story.

Characteristics of Scenic Form:
1. The reader has a sense of events taking place in real time.

2. The focus is up close and personal and gives a subjective viewpoint.
3. The pace is on the same level which we experience as human beings.
4. The degree of detail is very high.

Characteristics of Narrative Form:
1. The viewpoint is very objective and allows for generalizations.
2. Time can be compressed to cover periods as long as years or months or anything else for that matter.
3. The degree of detail is usually low with the general sense of things being more important than the specifics.
4. The reader gets the sense of being an omniscient viewer of events taking place rather than as a participant.

WEEK 26
MOVEMENT

Movement is the essence of a story and what differentiates it from an essay or a non-fiction work. Fiction has movement because in fiction we recreate a sense of time by giving to things an order of progression and a temporal notion of before and after and cause and effect. Beginning writers often forget to do this and the result is a hodge-podge of essay or conversation without any meaningful progression. Thus, learning how to implement movement within a story is one of the first hurdles to becoming a writer of fiction.

Movement can take place in a variety of ways in fiction. It may be helpful to review each of these ways and discuss how they differ from one another. It is important to understand that most fiction will involve many types of movement, if not all of them.

Types of Movement

1. Temporal – Temporal movement is that which is characterized by before and after or the past and the future. Temporal movement is the device most often employed in fiction. Writers simulate this by giving dates to certain events that take place in the fictional world or making it clear in the prose that time is passing as the book unfolds.

2. Spatial – Spatial movement is movement which takes place over a geographical area. This often occurs in "quest" or "adventure" type stories where the hero is in one location and must through the course of the book travel to another location whereupon he can accomplish his or her goal. Spatial movement is the easiest to write and comes natural to most writers since it allows them to explore different places and thus through description bring those places to life.

3. Psychological – Psychological movement is the movement that occurs in a character from a growth perspective (or dissolution). Essentially the writer is

showing the character change in response to the events that take place in the book. This type of movement is one of the hardest to portray and is often difficult for the beginning writer. The key is that the change in the character must be in response to a stimulus. Without the causal connection the sense of movement is lost. It should be noted that there are a vast number of psychological movements possible. Some of these are of the following variety: happiness to sadness, bravery to fear, comedy to tragedy, sanity to insanity, pleasure to pain, trust to distrust, evil to good, etc.

4. Relationship Movement – Relationship movement is really a subtype of psychological movement but because of its frequency of use it is best discussed separately. Relationships move by characters becoming close or falling apart on an emotional level. Note that this can also take place on a physical level as well. Most stories develop this movement in relation to falling in or out of love. By simulating this, the writer is able to give a sense of movement to the story.

The above gives a rudimentary understanding of the various types of movement which can take place in the story. A future section will cover each of these types in detail as well as show examples of how they can be implemented in fiction. It may be helpful to take notes when reading a book as to the various types of movement taking place and how the writer characterizes it through writing techniques.

WEEK 27
AFTER THE FIRST DRAFT

Okay, you have completed the first draft and you have decided it is terrible. No, not just terrible but virtually unreadable. If it wasn't for the fact that you wrote it you would burn it. If that is your feeling then read on as we figure out how to make it something respectable.

Let's first of all discuss the possible problems that you could be having with your first draft. Each of them will require a unique solution. We will discuss each problem with a solution followed immediately thereafter.

Problem #1) *The novel has no style or it is very unappealing to read*. This is the hardest problem to deal with because it requires a substantial rewrite of everything you have written. This is the worst problem you can encounter. The way this is solved is by first of all finding a style that works for you from authors you frequently read and then try and mimic that style while writing. This will take some practice. But if you can do it, it will ensure that your book is much more readable. Take apart a paragraph or a chapter of your favorite author and notice how and when he uses descriptions and the ratio of descriptions to action. Use this knowledge in the writing of your own chapter. It will be slow going at first but with time you will pick up speed. Try to match descriptions your favorite author uses with those in your book. Use his word choice patterns and style liberally. This doesn't mean you copy him – it means that you write as inspired by him or her. The truth is that by simply adding several good sentences in a paragraph you make the entire work much more readable. So the thing to do is to go through and do this with each chapter and each paragraph of your novel and the overall result will be much more readable.

Problem #2) *The scenes in the novel and/or the chapters are uninteresting and flat*. This is by far a more common problem. Here the problem is not the writing so much as it is the scene choice. The solution here is to simply go back to the overall story outline and rethink the scene choices and the chapter choices. Somehow you have to tell your story in scenes and these scenes must be interesting and draw the reader into the story. If your scenes are failing to do this then you need to rethink them and come up with something else. Find scenes that are exciting and have their own beginning, middle and end. Scenes that are surprising and interesting. If you have scenes that do all of these things then your readers will be enthralled in your story.

Problem #3) *The characters are flat and unappealing to the reader.* The reader is not attached to the lead character or finds them uninteresting. If this is the case then we know that everything the reader thinks about your character is a result of what you wrote about them. Therefore, go back and find all the scenes in which this character was described and see if you can find a way to do it differently. Find a way to bring them more to life. Look at how they say things and see if you can make them say things differently. Look at what they do and see if you can adjust this at all. Use different descriptions for them. Use different words to describe them through friends and acquaintances in the story. It is alright if the reader does not like your character as long as they find them interesting. Uninteresting characters are the kiss of death for a story. Avoid them at all costs.

Problem #4) *The dialogue is awkward.* This is something that must be fixed. This is a rather difficult area for the beginning writer. The thing to do is to go back into your document and find each location of dialogue and fix it by adding the appropriate format. This will require that you read the work of some writer you respect and copy the way he is doing his dialogue and then doing yours the same way.

Problem #5) *Awkward Transitions.* Transitions are a very important part of a novel. If the transition is not right then reading the novel will not be easy. Creating effective transitions is a craft and skill that comes with time. The best thing you can do is take your time and spend time thinking about each and every transition in your text. When you come up with a good transition then edit out the old transition and add the new one. Repeat as often as necessary.

WEEK 28
COMPONENTS OF FICTION

Every fiction book is comprised of the same basic elements. Most writers will be good in some of these elements and poor in others. Many people would assume that if someone is a good writer then they can write all components equally well. This is usually not the case. The writers who persevere and are eventually published will have to strengthen their writing skills in one or more of the specific components.

First of all it is helpful to understand the various components that make up any novel. These are the following:

1) Scene
    i. Scene is the basic unit of the novel. This is where the "action" takes place in real time in the mind of the reader. Scene can be made up of "things" happening which essentially means "causes and effects". Scene can also be made up of dialogue. Dialogue is the communication that takes place between the various characters. In terms of pacing dialogue and action typically read fast because they engage the reader.
2) Sequel
    i. Sequence is the internal reflections which takes place between scenes. Sequence is comprised of the various thought and emotions of the characters in the story. Sequel always reads very slowly in terms of pacing because it concerns feeling and logic versus action. Sequel often spans longer periods of time than action. This is because it usually takes time for the characters to process the events in a logical and emotional manner. For a sequel to be effective the characters must

form a decision which they in turn act upon, leading to the next scene. Sequels usually contain summary and often must have it if they are to be effective. Dialogue is often used for sequel. This entails allowing the characters to work out their emotions and thoughts via a discussion with another character.

3) Transition

    i. Transition is the writer's way of communicating to the reader that there has been a change in time, place or viewpoint. It usually only comprises a line or two but is necessary for the reader to properly understand the story.

Understanding what these basic story components are and how to write them is the basic task of every aspiring writer. As mentioned above some writers will naturally excel in one particular component and need to work to write the others well. As with anything practice makes perfect and the better the writer understands the tools the more effective will be the practice.

WEEK 29
THE POWER OF OPPOSITES

One important craft to cultivate is using opposites to enhance the meaning and the power of your writing. The way to use an opposite to enhance a story or section of prose is to first of all identify the core subject, theme or emotion that you are seeking to display and then identify its opposite with the objective of using it to illustrate the particular point you are attempting to make.

The best way to understand this technique is to illustrate an example:

Let us imagine that we are writing a horror novel where the key scene revolves around a deep seated fear or insecurity which we are attempting to evoke in the reader. Perhaps we have the scene taking place in a typical suburban neighborhood in the middle of the afternoon – not likely to be a very fearsome situation. Thus are objective is to pain a picture that connects with fear or insecurity in the heart of the reader. The original prose is as follows:

"Marjorie loved the way the afternoon breeze filtered its way through the garden when she was working in it this time of day. The way the flowers swayed evoked in her a sense of nostalgia as she often thought of helping her parents work in a similar garden many years ago. Suddenly she heard a door slam coming from the direction of her house. She couldn't imagine what would be making that noise since she was the only one home – John wouldn't be back from work for hours. She turned around and…"

Thus you can see we have a typical scene in which we are given a woman working in a garden who is about to witness some event that will change the complexion of the scene. What is needed here are some vague ominous observations that can bring out the contrast in the scene. We will use opposites to bring about this effect. First of all we will examine the basic symbols we are working at and then try to engage their opposite meanings for purpose of alliteration.

Word	Meaning	Opposite
Garden	Cultivated, Tame	Wild, unwieldy
Parents	Protection, Safety	Offenders, threats

Okay now that we have two symbols we can work with we will seek to utilize them in enhancing the fearfullness of the scene.

"Marjorie loved the way the afternoon breeze filtered its way through the garden when she was working this time of day though she couldn't help notice the way it rearranged the helpless daisies so that their efforts of reaching the sun were meaningless. Still, the way they swayed evoked in her a sense of nostalgia as she often thought of helping her parents work in a similar garden many years ago. Those thoughts were not without their own danger though as they too easily made her recall the swiftness with which life can change and things you depend on can quickly dissolve"

This is a poor example but if you can look past the ineloquent writing style you can see how the added observations create a more menacing air about the entire scene. The key to evoking emotion or a response is never in the scene itself but instead in what is being focused on. Knowing this one can easily see how a perfectly tranquil scene can become menacing very quickly. The art of writing fiction is in choosing what to focus on and how to convey the information. All the rest is just details.

WEEK 30
GOING FROM FIRST DRAFT TO SECOND DRAFT

Learning how to properly edit and revise your own writing is tantamount to the hidden secret of really becoming a writer. It is this skill that more often than not separates the amateur from the pro. And it is also a decidedly difficult skill for most to learn. It involves a division of yourself into two parts – the editor part and the writer part. This division is much easier said than done. Let's look at the process in detail.

Writing requires the skill of imagination and a flair for using words to build worlds. Obviously some have more of this skill than others. Writing engages the senses and the unconscious part of the brain to conjure a believable story and sequence of events ex nihlo. Many writers will attest to the fact that the writerly side of a writer often seems like an entirely separate personality with a mind of its own.

Editing requires a completely different skill set. Editing requires that an individual be able to read "fresh" and compare what he reads versus other similar stories and determine what works and what does not. Editing is a process of selection. The key is that the writer must think abstractly in the sense that every sentence is measured against the thousands of other possible ways it could be formed and said. The editor then must decide whether or not the sentence passes muster based on the internal criteria of comparison to other works. Writing is like capturing an unknown wild animal you hope to eventually tame. During the writing stage you are just doing all you can to get it on paper. Afterwards you realize that the editing stage is a completely different ballgame and much of what you wrote is unusable or poorly written. What then?

Then you edit. You go back and you discard the original sentence by sentence or chapter by chapter and you give it another go. You use the old standby which geniuses have used since time memorial – you try as many ways as it takes until you finally click on one that works. Depending on your skill as a writer this process may take days, weeks, months, years or lifetimes.

The complete uniqueness of this particular skill set cannot be emphasized enough. It is a "facet" of the writing process that must be learned. Just like plotting/story development, characterization, description or any other aspect of writing. Your level of discernment and your ability to improvise are the keys to success during this particular process of the writing endeavor. Thus, you are encouraged to be inexhaustible, unscrupulous, critical and never tiring. If you can do each of those just a little bit you might turn a mess into a masterpiece.

WEEK 31
OUTLINING

Before you ever write a word of a novel or a non-fiction project you should have on paper a plan. This means that you already know the scenes and what order they are in for a story and the general information about the characters and places which will populate the story.

Now I am sure that many are already vehemently protesting this notion and giving examples of great writers who never use an outline. Is this true? Partially. Those who claim to write freeform are essentially doing the outlining process as they write OR they have already done so in their head. Some of us prefer to have the outline in front of us on paper or to work through it before we actually begin writing. Regardless of which you prefer, the necessity of knowing what you are going to write before you write it should be apparent to anyone.

So the question becomes what must be planned – or what exactly must you know – before beginning the process? I would suggest the following:

1) The Central Character(s) – There are two schools of story development: those who begin with a character and those who begin with an event or situation. I will cover the situation approach next. For now, just think about envisioning your main character and more importantly WHAT HE WANTS and WHAT IS KEEPING HIM FROM IT. This is the essence of conflict and any character without conflict is a boring character and boring characters don't deserve to have book written about them. How much do you need to know about a character? You need to know enough to make him interesting and to find out more you have to find out what it is that makes people interesting. The answer to that is the reason there are enough book genres and story types to make a writers head spin. Find what interests you and then write from there. If you continue you will

eventually find your audience who will be enthralled by the same type of people and situations.

2) The Situation – This could be called the situation or the conflict or the inciting incident or any number of applicable terms that essentially mean the same thing: WHAT HAPPENS and WHY IT IS IMPORTANT. This is a loose description that encompasses both character dramas as well as novels focused in action that takes place in the physical world. How much do you need to know? Sometimes it is simply enough to know that some dark and stormy night a stranger shows up at a castle. A book can bloom from something simply as that and naturally characters will follow.

3) The "World" – The word "world" is a very lose description of what is better understood as the environment or backdrop against which the "movement" takes place. The world may be a foreign culture or an alien civilization or even the delusions someone experiences in everyday life. Regardless of which, you need to know enough about "it" to be able to describe it and make it believable for your reader. Not only that but you must make it interesting too. And to know what will make it interesting, more excavation is required. As above, you need to find out what interests you.

4) The "Movement" – Movement is the   quid pro quo of entertainment. It is the state of change which makes life interesting and thus we demand movement in our entertainment. Music has rhythms and tempos and stories have incidents and events. Both provide the change which makes the piece interesting. Thus, you need to know in general how the change will occur. As they say though, the devil is in the details. Stephen King creates change by introducing a maniacal and homicidal fan to a writer (see Misery) while David Mitchell introduces change by a characters realization that he has a ghost living with him (see Ghostwritten).

5) The "Meaning" or the "Message" – Some may protest by saying entertainment does not need a message. I counter by saying the decision that there is no meaning

or message is a message by itself. Think upon this yourself and come to your own conclusions.

WEEK 32
TRACKING

Tracking your production in some manner is an absolute necessity in pursuing a professional writing career. The reason tracking is important is that it makes you accountable (if only to yourself) and it provides you with a way to assess your performance. Thus, if you get to a point of desperation two years into your writing career you can look back and see exactly how much work you have put into the endeavor. Most of the time we only get out of something what we have put into it and if we are disappointed with the results it probably means we need to work harder and smarter.

The best method for tracking is to simply take a word count of all writing produced in a given day. However, for those who seek to write fiction it is only fictional material that should be counted. For those who write non-fiction, it should only be writing submitted for publication. Above and beyond these categories many writers keep a journal but by no means should this be counted as part of your word totals for a given day.

Another aspect of tracking is setting goals. This topic is covered in further detail later in the book but for now, it is important to say that every writer should have a specific word count in mind as a goal. One thousand words a day is a good amount that will stretch the average writer somewhat while at the same time being brief enough that they can not feel daunted.

Once you have tracked for a certain period of time it is helpful to go back and analyze the information to see what you can learn about your writing habits. You may find that you typically start strong in the beginning of a month and then fall off toward the end. If so, then perhaps you can take steps to remedy this situation by rearranging your work schedule. Look for patterns on particular days or on monthly cycles. See where and when you do your best work so you can be prepared to schedule your most important projects during that time.

One last aspect of tracking is to write with the end in mind. This means that you should have an ongoing record of projects completed. Whether those completions are books, articles or screenplays you should have some goal as to how often and how many you seek to complete in a given period of time. For example, my personal goal is to complete at least one novel and one screenplay a year. Knowing this, I can look back and see something that stands as a testament to my progress as a writer for any given year. Only by continuing to produce will you continue to improve.

WEEK 33
GETTING PAST THE FLUFF

There is much to be said for volume of output. It may be the biggest factor in determining eventual success in the field of writing. The simple truth is that those who produce more material eventually produce better material on average than those who produce less material. This applies to screenplays, novels, non-fiction, articles, blogs and practically any other form of writing.

Why do we find this to be the case? It is probably a number of factors. Some general benefits of producing more are the following:

- Those who produce more get better because of more practice.
- Those who produce more are able to get past their early "beginner" works and move on to those of better merit.
- Those who produce more are also read more and as a result they get more feedback which allows them to gain skill.
- Those who produce more are better equipped to get past places where a lower volume writer might get stuck – mainly because writing has become a habit.
- Those who produce more have my confidence in their ability which always translates into better writing.
- Those who produce more tend to be better acclimated to criticism and be able to incorporate it and move on rather than let it bother them.

The above are just some of the reasons high-volume writers have more success than those who write sparingly. If nothing else, sheer volume allows you to get past the fluff to the things you really want to say. And that may be the best reason of all to write more instead of less.

WEEK 34
DISCOURAGEMENT

Discouragement is a fact of life and one we must deal with constructively if we are ever to make progress. This is true in writing just as it is in everything else. Thus, it helps to accept that you will become discouraged somewhere along the journey of becoming a writer. It will happen. The only question is when. Knowing this, it is important to understand how to handle it and what to learn from it and how to get past it.

Discouragement is usually a good sign. Often it comes from ourselves and our own evaluation of our progress or lack thereof. Other times it will come from the comments from somebody else – perhaps a partner or another writer. Many times the evaluation we make ourselves or that somebody else makes will be accurate. Then we are forced to accept the fact that we are not as far along as we would like to be and our writing is not at the level we expected. Once we can accept this and understand that it is part of the process which EVERY writer goes through then we can begin to move forward.

There are certain things you can do when you find yourself in the midst of discouragement about your writing. One of the first things to do is to simply remind yourself that all writers go through this at some point regardless of their talent level. It is a result of having high expectations and human failings. Knowing that it is common to all writers it is helpful to remind yourself that the good writers get past these times and continue to write and to improve. You will not make any improvement if you cease writing. Improvement only comes from practice and trying new things. Thus, feel the emotion and then begin writing again. By actively writing you will eventually get past the point of discouragement.

For those who find themselves blocked by discouragement, it may be helpful to read a few books on the subject to help you feel better about where you are on the journey of becoming a writer. Two very helpful books, whether you are a neophyte or a veteran, are the following books by Ralph Keyes:

1. **The Courage to Write** – Henry Holt Publishing. ISBN 0-8050-3189-8
2. **The Writer's Book of Hope** – Owl Books. ISBN 0-8050-7235-7

WEEK 35
A READERSHIP: Alternative Publishing

The end objective of every writer is to gain a readership – people who love and appreciate your style and your subject matter. In the end this is what it is all about. Good writing is a very nebulous term that in the end can only be measured in terms readers and response. There have been numerous books throughout the history of publishing that were characterized as being written poorly that still managed to reach the best seller list and connect with an audience. All of this should be encouraging to those who still want to write despite criticism. If you keep writing you WILL find an audience. It just takes time and perseverance.

How do you go about finding an audience? Well, with the internet the ability to do that has expanded greatly. The traditional blog is most certainly an alternative publishing route. There have been numerous writers who began something as a blog which eventually lead to a bonafide publishing deal. The key is to attract a readership and to "market" it to some extent. After that you are left to depend on response and word of mouth to drive new readers to your writing.

Those who don't have a blog are not without alternatives. There is always the self-publishing route which has spawned numerous successes and continues to do so on a regular basis. Many books started out self-published before going on to become best sellers with a reputable publishing house. Even if a publisher doesn't think your writing has merit they will listen to readers who buy enough of your books to make them take notice. Thus, by self-publishing you can prove that there is a place for your work and that there are readers who will gladly pay money to read what you write. In the end that is all I writer can ask for.

Wherever you are in your writing career it is wise to explore other avenues of gaining a readership. Blogs, newsletters, bulletin boards, serial fiction and many others are all acceptable

ways of getting your work in front of the people who matter –
the readers.

Go to any large bookstore and take a look at the numerous
categories and sections. You will find a category for almost any
type of book. If you take the time and look through the
individual books making up a section you will probably find a
large variety of styles and techniques. The point of this is to
show the large variety of readers out there. There are literally
enough readers in the world that if you look hard enough and
long enough you will find readers for the type of books you
write.

So given the above there is no reason you can't find an audience
and get your work in front of that audience. The alternative
publishing methods are accessible to most anyone now and the
internet makes access to reading audiences easier than anytime
in the history of the written word. This should be encouraging
news to those who love to write. If you write it, they will read
it eventually in one format or the other.

WEEK 36
CAUSE AND EFFECT

One of the chief problems in the early works of the average
writer is an inadequate understanding of cause and effect in
story structure. Often the first novel will be found to diverge
into tangents of only congenial relation to the story – to the
detriment to the story. This usually happens because the author
failed to understand the causal connection between the
events/scenes portrayed in the book. Fortunately, this is less of
a problem in screenplays since the average film length creates a
requirement on the part of the writer to cut all but the most
necessary scenes when writing the script.

Cause and effect is best utilized in the early development
process of crafting a story. Often, when done after the fact it
ends up with the writer realizing a great deal of his or her novel
is irrelevant and needs to be sacrificed for the good of the
whole. This is never a pleasant experience. After all, who
wants to spend two weeks researching and writing an involved
discussion of the Orchid only to find it cut in the end anyway?
Not many of us have the time or fortitude to deal with such
things. Thus, understanding your story from a cause/effect
point of view is recommended as an early exercise BEFORE
you ever begin the process of writing the story.

It takes a while before you realize just how important
cause/effect is as a writer. Often the first few attempts at a
novel or screenplay (usually unsuccessful) will result in many
loose ends that are insufficiently resolved by the time the story
reaches the climax. Or on the converse the story will be devoid
of conflict entirely and will end up being a patchwork of loosely
related slice-of-life style portraits that fail to generate enough
drama to sustain interest. All of these problems can be solved
by a thorough understanding of the cause/effect connection
between each scene within your story. Not only that but often it
will point you toward scenes that have not been included that
are necessary for your story to work successfully.

So, the question you are probably asking is how do you go about this process? While it seems obvious and may be to some, it does help to actually illustrate the technique being used. Thus, the example below gives a full explanation of the method illustrating the entire process for a series of 4 scenes. Of course when it comes to actually working with your own story you want to proceed all the way from the end to the beginning (and yes you should work in reverse!). For those seeking a fuller explanation of the process as well as other insights to the story development process the book "Writing a Great Movie" by Jeff Kitchen is highly recommended. Jeff is a classically trained dramatist that does a wonderful job of explaining many of the tricks in crafting a quality dramatic storyline.

WEEK 37
WHEN SHOULD YOU BEGIN WRITING

Figuring out when you should actually start writing a story is not as easy as it seems. Legions are those who have started on a story too early only to find their idea was only half formed and not properly developed. On the other hand there are many who develop a story way past the point that they should with the end result being a lack of excitement or passion for the story after so much research. Somewhere between these two fine lines is the proper time to begin a story. We will discuss some ways you can tell when you are ready to actually begin writing.

Research is certainly important and often it is the difference between a high quality book and a low quality book. The good writers take their time to research the important facets of the story to make sure they have everything right. They especially pay attention to such details as technology, forensics, science, etc. When you read books by these types of authors it is very easy to tell how much work they have done. You actually learn something about a subject you knew nothing about before you read the book. Thus we can conclude that research is certainly a very important aspect of writing a high quality book. However, the important question is when do you stop researching and start writing?

The best indication that you can begin writing is when you have researched all the major aspects of the central storyline. This is the primary reason for research. You have to make sure the logic in your storyline is consistent and accurate and not ruined by some unresearched fact about forensics or some other obscure area of life. The best thing you can do is to ask yourself what are the various subjects that need to be researched that your plot is dependent upon. One writer had the experience of writing almost ¾'s of a book on a runaway nuclear missile before he found out that the technology just did not work as he had anticipated. In fact it rendered the whole story impossible and he was forced to discard a years worth of work. This could have been avoided if he had researched the subject up front and found out to begin with that his premise was logically flawed. So in conclusion the proper time to quit researching is when you have worked out any possible problems with the primary plot. Most of the subplot issues will be fixable or changeable so there is no need to worry about them until after the first draft.

Outlining is another aspect of "prewriting" that writers have vastly different opinions on. However regardless of which school you hold to (the "plot it and write school" or the "just write it" school) a good rule of thumb is to leave some flexibility within your outline so that you can deviate from the story if the muse feels it necessary. Another important thing to remember is to not research or outline so much that you lose your passion and excitement for the story you want to tell. Stop before that happens and you can be certain that excitement will flow thorough to the book.

WEEK 38
ORGANIZATION

A writer must learn how to organize material if he or she is to find some amount of success. Disorganization has proven to be the Achilles heel for numerous writers and it has often be the difference between failure and success. Organization is important in all stages of the writing process and is not something exclusive to the writing of the manuscript itself. Without organization most, if not all projects will be doomed to fail.

Let's discuss several areas in which a writer must have a solid system of organization:

Area 1 – Future Projects

The first step in a writers system of organization begins with ideas which will eventually become projects. The writer must have some method by which new ideas are organized and through which a select number of those ideas move forward to official writing projects. The best method for this stage is to simply have a folder or file system with a designated area for each unique idea. This will allow you to make notes and add to the compiled material as time goes on.

Area 2 – Current Projects

The writer must have some method of organizing active projects. Ideally there should be several designated area including: general notes/ characters / plot / background material / scene idea / etc. Every writer will find a different method by which they naturally organize their projects. The important thing to do is to keep the material together and in some semblance of order.

Area 3 – Assignments

Most writers will do some freelance work on assignment in addition to their own projects. It is important that these be organized and scheduled so that deadlines are met on time without undue delay.

Area 4 – Archived Material

At some point most of us experience the loss of files and at times entire manuscripts. The best method of prevention against this disaster is to make regular backups so that if it does occur you can recover the most recent versions of existing documents. The handiest method is to use a CD-R or DVD-R but hard copy works just as well for the technophobes among us. The important thing is to have a system for archiving material regardless of what method you use.

The above systems are the minimum for a working writer. Some writers have other methods which they use to stay productive and efficient. Ask around and see what others are using and incorporate their methods if you find them helpful. Organization is always the first step on the road to writing success!

WEEK 39
DEDICATION

Above all the most important trait in becoming a writer is dedication to writing. You must be dedicated to the act of putting words down on paper. Not reading, not outlining, not journaling but actually writing fictional accounts of things down on paper. Without this nothing will get accomplished. There are many who find themselves loving the idea of being a writer more than the actual writing. This cannot be you. If you want to be a writer you simply must write there is no way around it.

There is an additional problem for some people. These are the people who don't have a problem with writing per se but instead have a problem with what they write. Perhaps their scenes are not flowing like they should, or they can't get past the organization stage or some other writing related problem. For these people the key is to figure out what it is you are doing wrong and then correct it. It takes years for some to have the insight necessary to make the leap. Thus you cannot give up hope. If you are having problems with one aspect of writing then the best you can do is to simply study that particular aspect in hopes that you eventually discover what it is you are doing wrong. With time, patience and persistence you should overcome the problem.

Dedication ensures that you won't give up when you realize that the first novel you written is not worthy of the paper it is printed on. It also means you will dig in and try again and try to get the next one right or at least make it better. Dedication ensures you are dedicated to the task of writing itself more so than you are the satisfaction of having written. Dedication means you realize you are on a never-ending quest of conquering a mountain of which you can never reach the summit. You must keep on and you must keep at it and you must keep trying. Only by doing these things will you reach your goal.

WEEK 40
IMPROVING AS A WRITER

How does a writer improve?

If you read the biography of any number of writers you will find that most of them arrive after a number of years of honing their craft. This honing takes place through sheer volume and experimentation for most of them. It has been noted that it takes the average writer an entire nine years from the moment he or she becomes serious about the craft to the moment in which they are finally published. That is nine years of writing and writing and writing without any noticeable success other than that in the writers own mind. This "apprenticeship" period, more than anything else determines the overall success or failure of the writer later in life. Without diligent, hard and persistent work the writer will be without the skills necessary to elevate his craft to a form of art. With it, he or she establishes the foundation for eventual success.

But how does a writer actually acquire these necessary skills? How is it he or she should spend his "formative time" in the trenches? Because ever person is different there are a variety of different ways in which a writer can improve. The success of any particular method depends on the preferred learning style of the writer. Essentially, the writer must know how he or she learns and then apply that particular method to the art of writing. However, regardless of the method used in the end a writer can mature only through repetition, practice and becoming better at the thing which he does – mainly writing or telling stories.

What are the specific methods? They are a many. A writer can improve by learning what he or she is doing wrong and correcting it. A writer can improve by seeing others do it well and copying it. A writer can improve by experimentation and feedback. A writer can improve by telling stories verbally. A writer can improve by simply reading and soaking up the methods of other writers. A writer can improve through sheer experimentation. The methods are many. However, the bottom line is that a writer must improve by practice, practice, practice. In the end word count becomes the Holy Grail of the apprentice writer.

The key is to simply try as many and varied methods as it takes for you to begin making progress. Keep trying, keep writing and keep improving. Those are the essentials for success. If you work harder and longer than the average person you will eventually achieve your goal. That is the only guarantee in the pursuit of art. Time must be invested. Improvements must be made.

WEEK 41
OBSERVATION

The one trait that seems to define the ability to write is that of observation. Most would-be or actual writers have a very unique ability and desire to observe the world around them. There have been exceptions to this fact. There have been many writers like Hemmingway, who seek out experience on a first hand basis instead of observing it solely.

Observation isn't just the quality of watching something take place. Observing also has a quality of subjectivity to it – in that the WAY something is observed is unique to the observer – or the writer. Thus, two great writers will observe things in totally unique ways. Each will focus on particular aspects of the scene unfolding and find meaning in unique ways. Thus, a writer must cultivate his unique manner of observing and find a way to get it in words and on paper so that the experience can be transmitted to a reader. Essentially this is the magic that takes place in the end; a reader through your words and scenes is able to experience your perception of events that took place either in reality or imagination.

Observation can be improved by practice. Try to spend an entire afternoon simply watching the world around you. Find details that are beyond the realm of the conventional eye. Find meaning in places one would not normally find it. Let the world open itself up to you and tell you what it would like to tell you. If you can learn to listen to the voice of the world and the voice of your imagination then you are well on your way to becoming a writer.

The devil is in the details – always. Thus, it is the small things which you focus on in a description that make the biggest difference. Everyone is able to transmit the details of what took plays through the eyes only. But those who learn to see beyond the eyes are few and far between. So you must learn to see with more than your eyes and you must learn to get this experience down on paper so that the scene taking place before the eyes is enhanced and illuminated by those things taking place beyond them.

WEEK 42
HOW TO BEGIN

Learning how to write is a process just like anything else. However, there are certain levels of mastery that one should take in stride and in a certain order because one talent builds upon the others. Thus, it is recommended that the writer start with scenes, then progress to shorts and then to novellas and finally to novels. This progression ensures that you learn all vital aspects of the craft and do not become frustrated attempting something which is beyond your capability to early in the learning cycle.

The progression above is based on the logic of storytelling. The scene is the basic component of all forms of drama. Thus the very first challenge is to craft exciting, believable and entertaining scenes in various manners. Try one that is derived of action, another of dialogue and another of reflection. Once the scene has been mastered then it is on to the short.

The short is made up of scenes. In some rare cases it is made up of a single scene but this is the exception. Far more common is the short that is made up of several scenes all tied together by reflection or introspection on the part of the main character or the author. Examine some shorts and determine the layout of their component parts. This will assist you in learning what is needed in creating your own short story. After you have mastered the short form then you should take the next step toward the novella.

The novella is the next step on the ladder of scope in writing fiction. The novella is approximately 50,000 words give or take, and for the most part comprised of one central movement or storyline. There is usually poignancy to the short and the distinction of subtlety that the form lends itself to. Writing a novella is best approached by studying some of the better ones and then understanding how they use the same basic components to build the story. "The Old Man and The Sea" is a fine example. The opening gives an introduction to the character which is followed by scene consisting of primarily dialogue. The rest of the story builds on these same components in unveiling the drama taking place and the essential movement of the story.

The novel is the last and greatest of the dramatic forms of literature. Length and depth are two characteristics that mark it separate from its forebears. The scene is a sprint, the novella is a middle distance race and the novel is a marathon. Though each requires the same basic components they are each subtlety and artistically different and require separate talents and focus. The writer should stay away from the novella until he or she has mastered the prior art forms first. Doing so will prevent unnecessary frustration which often takes place in the first, second or third failed attempt at a novel.

This series of artistic progressions should create a sound foundation for a writing career if it is adhered to in a disciplinary fashion. The mastering of the small steps individually leads to the mastering of the form in general. As long as that is remembered and adhered to then the rest will take care of itself.

WEEK 43
THE ENDING

An ending must accomplish a variety of things: it must successfully resolve the main storyline (unless you specifically want an ambiguous ending); it must resolve any unanswered questions that remain in the mind of the audience (what happened to that gun from the first act anyway?); it must give the reader/viewer a sense that "justice" has been served (or that it has not in antiplots); it must generate the appropriate emotional response and lastly it must be consistent with and enhance the theme dealt with throughout the earlier part of the story.

Writing a good ending is an art just like writing a good beginning. Some beginnings and endings are written well enough that they resonate in the mind of the viewer/reader long after the experience of the story is over. These are the kind of endings one should hope to write, realizing that they are very difficult to do without practice and editing.

It is important to keep in mind that any story may have any number of endings. Some will be implausible, some will be unlikely, some will not be right, some will never be believed, some will just feel wrong and many will be "passable" without achieving the effect one would really like. It is easy to forget this when writing or when editing an already completed story. Once we have written a certain ending we tend to keep ourselves in that particular box without looking for further ideas and inspiration that may in fact be better than our original choice. Sometimes the best endings come from keeping an open mind and continuing to plow the field of possibilities. Just because you have one that works there is no reason to limit yourself to staying with it and believing there is nothing better out there. Keep reaching and keep trying. You never know what you might come up with.

The ending should also have some sort of resonance and mirroring of the opening. This is not a requirement but it is a nice effect that when achieved can give the entire story a quality of harmony that would otherwise not exist. We all know the stories where a character opens a story in a bar and then at the conclusion finds himself or herself in the same bar, albeit wiser and worse the wear from the events which took place in the interval.

A good ending is an art that requires the most of a writer's talent. Try not to settle for the expected ending but instead reach for something that the audience had not anticipated. More than anything else a story should surprise and expand boundaries. A cliché ending will never do this but a unique and inventive one does it every time.

WEEK 44
PACING

Pacing can vary widely in published novels. It can range all the way from the breakneck speed of an action/adventure novel to the more leisurely pace of a coming of age story. What determines pace? Pace is the frequency with plot changes which are integral to the story take place on the pages. Some places focus on primarily physical action while others focus on changes in the mental landscape. The important point though is that your audience will require some "change" to take place on a fairly regular basis or they will lose interest.

Genre will dictate pace more than anything else. Most genres have readers with well-defined expectations in terms of action and basic plot material. Fantasy readers want to see the occasional battle followed by diplomacy. Military stories expect to read about the fights interspersed with armed forces meetings and base dynamics. Romances want to see rendezvous between the focal characters in between personal struggles of the protagonist. Of course knowing what the expectations of a particular genre are is only half the battle. One must still determine what is right for the story in terms of the time divided between action and summary material (sequel/reflection).

To better grasp pacing try the following: Pick up whatever novel you would like and read a short section consisting of mainly dialogue. After you finish, find a comparable section of non-dialogue and read it. Afterward, reflect on which reads faster and seems to take place at a quicker pace. By far, dialogue reads fast and increases the pacing of a story. Thus, one quick solution to quickening the pace is to simply have more scenes which are dialogue heavy. Though dialogue isn't action in a primary sense it does read that way for the average reader. This is because we are used to conversation and language and can quickly digest exactly what is taking place. Compare this to the average action scene where the reader has to mentally construct the events taking place in order to fully understand what the writer is communicating. Simply put, dialogue is faster.

Another aspect of pacing is sentence and paragraph construction. If you reflect on the above paragraphs you will find that they are not fast in terms of pacing. They consist of long sentences which are all placed one after the other without any breaks. This is one method of slowing down the pace of a story. Simply, use longer sentences and don't paragraph indent as often. Compare the above to the following:

Pacing is the speed at which a reader devours your book.

Short sentences quicken the pace.

Long sentences increase it.

Albeit, this is a very bad example but you should get the basic idea that pacing can be controlled by the writer using sentence length, word choice and paragraph indention. Upon completion of a novel the writer should give it to a trusted reader for feedback on pacing. Depending on the answer the task is then to either leave it as is or speed it up or slow it down with the tools mentioned above.

WEEK 45
WHY READERS READ

This seems elementary but truly it is a very important principle to understand and one that is unfortunately lost on many beginning writers. The simple answer is this – A writer reads to see what happens next. This can be expanded to include other similar answers such as – to find out what happened, to see why something occurred, to see what happened to a character, etc. The important thing to take away from all of this is that in the end it is the QUESTION that drives the story forward or to put it another way, it is what we don't know that makes us continue to read.

So why is this so important? It is important for the simple fact that as a beginning writer the first instinct is to tell EVERYTHING there is to tell in a scene or a sequence. As a result we have a great deal of interesting information and perhaps even captivating dialogue and situations but in the end there is no incentive left for the reader to continue reading. The reader already knows everything there is to know. Why should he or she continue reading your story? In the end it is what is not said or not explained or not told that is the most important element of the story! It is what we don't say that is more important than what we do say.

Instinctively, because we have all heard enough stories and told enough ourselves, we will often coach the story in such a way that we withhold information until a key point. However, more often than not this instinct is not good enough to instill the proper amount of drama and anticipation into a long form such as a novel or a screenplay. Our instinct is usually sufficient for a short story and perhaps even a novella but when it comes to a novel it is often necessary to actively plan the process by which information is revealed. If you reveal too much too soon then just like a bad joke, the story will fall flat. However, if you create anticipation and whet the reader's appetite and make them want to know more and feed them a little at a time over a course of a series of chapters or a hundred pages or so then in the end you have done your job and the reader will walk away with a rewarding experience.

What are the elements that a reader might want to know about that can create this sense of curiosity and anticipation?

1. Who killed Mr. Robinson? – This is the crux of the murder plot. We see a dead person and we instinctively want to know who did it so justice can be served.
2. Why is the situation like it is? – This is a broad generalization for all stories in which a unique person or circumstance is presented that begs the question – why are things the way they are?
3. Will Jack and Jill get together? – This is the key to all romances and romantic comedies. We are given two likeable and charismatic main characters and our next inclination is to see if these two people, who are obviously deserving of one another, have the chance to develop a romantic relationship.
4. Will the bad guys be defeated? – These types of stories carry across many genres. Essentially a bad guy(s) is presented committing horrible acts in an initial scene which is followed by the presentation of a "good guy" character. Our natural instinct is for the good guy to defeat the bad guy.
5. Will disaster be averted? – This scenario is often presented in such a way that an impending disaster is foretold or actually begins to take place upsetting the precarious balance of the world. The follow up usually presents a series of characters or character that we soon find ourselves rooting for and hoping that they might somehow avert the disaster or at the very least survive it.

Those are just a few brief examples of story questions that can drive a story forward. Of course there are many more. The key thing to take away from all of this is that it is the story question that drives the story and not the story answer. You should always delay answering story questions as long as possible and when you do give a story answer it should always be one that the audience/reader has not anticipated.

It is this key element that makes stories magical and provides the reader with the experience they long for.

WEEK 46
INTEGRATING INFORMATION AND EXPLORATION
INTO THE STORY (Part Two)

We are all creatures of novelty. We are driven by a desire for new information, experiences and automatically take notice of anything out of the ordinary. We are also problem solvers and organizers. Our very evolution has depended on all of these skills to keep us alive and allow us to occupy our place at the top of the food chain. These are not only important traits that have contributed to our success as a species but they are also the things we look for as a reader when we seek to be entertained.

As a writer, the biggest job you have is to keep the reader interested. While, what interests us in particular may vary from individual to individual, we can agree that as a whole it falls into one of the categories above. Not only are these the things that interest us readers but usually they are also the things that interest us as writers. Though the prosaic "autobiography" may be boring to most everyone else, it is our own way of making sense of our life and giving it some significance. Thus, even the most boring bionovel will still fall within the categories listed above. Let's examine each of these categories separately and discuss how they can be integrated into a story.

1) New Information – This falls under a number of categories. A location can be new information to somebody who hasn't been there. An intellectual discipline such as a branch of science, a unique job, a philosophy or a religion, a new language, a new understanding of the world; all of these things can be integrated into a story. The more you integrate information that the reader has not come across before the more they will be interested in what they are reading. However, this is only to a certain degree since at some point too much new information becomes confusing and can disorient us and disconnect us from the reading experience.

2) New Experiences – An experience is essentially a packet of information. However, for the sake of clarity we will discuss it separately. Life is too short for us to do everything we would like to do and we often find our dreams in life frustrated. Thus, for psychological satisfaction we often seek to experience the things we cannot do in reality vicariously through fiction. So in a nutshell, though we might not be able to travel to Mauritius, we can read about the experience of a fictional character that goes there and in a sense this satisfies the same need we had for the experience.

3) Problem Solving – Anytime we are presented a problem, whether it is in fiction or in real life, our automatic inclination is to attempt to solve it. We have been molded by our ability to reason through things and work out solutions. Thus, as writers, we know that simply by presenting a problem we can rely on the reader to seek a solution to it and to show some level of interest whether that interest is on a conscious level or not. The most important thing to remember is that our readers will naturally be interested in a problem and remain interested as long as there is a lack of a solution. We can use this information to our advantage when we ensure that conflict is heightened and problems are presented. However, we must always remember that to maintain interest we must delay the solution to the problem and add complications along the way.

4) Organizing – When there is chaos, the tendency is to create art. It is this inclination that guides our sense of beauty and our appreciation of art. When we are given information that is disjointed and incongruent we will automatically try to organize that information. This is why it is appealing to read something by authors such as James Joyce or Thomas Pincheon. These types of novels create a sense of confusion and chaos that we seek to organize and make sense of and because of that we continue to read until we feel we have made a somewhat coherent understanding of the information. This approach is not for everyone but even on a small

scale it can be used as a tool for maintaining reader interest by the enterprising fiction writer.

WEEK 47
PREWRITING THE FIRST DRAFT

There are many, many methods by which one can write a novel. In fact, there are probably as many methods as there are writers. What follows, is only one such method. Some will find it useful and others will find it useless. If it works for you then by all means use it but if it doesn't then quickly pass on to the next lesson. For what it's worth, this came to me in a dream. More than likely, the result of my subconscious regurgitating something I had read once in a book on writing a novel. Regardless, I had went to sleep contemplating the best way for me to write a novel and this is what came to me.

The first step in this method is to use a simple summary or outline of your proposed novel. Simple can mean just the beginning and the end if you so desire. You will be required to flesh out the rest of it as you go along so whatever you start with is fine. This method of novel writing works by iterations. The objective is to go deeper and more detailed with each iteration until you have completed the first draft. This method also utilizes both summary and scene and thus forces you to not only distinguish the difference between the two but also to actually go through and change your summaries into scenes.

After you have written the summary then you go through the next step, which is to bring the summary to life in scenic form. This is obviously the hardest step and it is easy to see a two paragraph summary turn into a fifteen page exegesis. Obviously you must retain reader interest so that you don't get too weighed down in detail but all in all the objective is just to flesh out the scene and turn the prewriting to actual writing.

What follows is an example of the method using two chapters – the beginning of a hypothetical novel as well as the ending:

Prewriting/Summary:
1. Beginning – A castle besot by storms and an all king contemplating a war that has gone bad. As he watches

the storm he is interrupted by a retainer who tells him of a strange visitor. The scene ends with the king watching the visitor arriving in the courtyard down below.

2. Ending – The king from earlier gazes at the ruins of his castle and contemplates the loss of all his people and his kingdom and his own position, now that of a lone warrior hoping to rail against the changes taking place that very well bring about the end of the world itself

As you can see the above summaries are simply paragraph notions of what is to take place within a given chapter. They are a bit more than an outline and for some it is best to actually write the outline first and then develop the summaries from the outline. The trick is to actually go through and do the summary for each scene just as above and then to go on to the next step which is the scene.

Scenes:

1. Beginning –

Galian spent his evenings watching the sea. He knew he found it comforting but he was unsure exactly why. Sometimes it was so still that it almost seemed made of glass, a great window to some long forgotten world. Other times, he would watch it rage with strength and fury as if some old god were mad at existence itself. Tonight was one of those nights.

He took a deep draw on his pipe and thought about time, fate and the roads which had brought him to this place, this point in existence and how one small change could have just as easily thrust him in a different direction. He sighed, realizing he was becoming contemplative, knowing that contemplation was a luxury of fools with time to spare and time was something he had little of.

He heard footsteps approaching behind him.

"Sire?" It was Beragon, his advisor. He knew he would prefer not to hear whatever it was he had to say.

"Yes," he replied.

101

"We have news from the Northern front. I fear it is not good news though."

"Be on with it."

"We lost two battalions, only a few escaped and they arrived a few hours ago."

He grimaced. This was not good news at all.

"We outnumbered the Kramaj five men to one. How could we have been defeated so easily?"

"I fear they were dealt with treacherously liege. The Kramaj poisoned the waters of the river; the river from which the troops drank. The ones that escaped were only able to do so because they were infirm and had to be fed by water kept aside for the healer."

He grimaced again and took another deep draw of his pipe.

"These Kramaj are unholy sire. They know not honor. They fight without morals, like the beasts." Beragon stated.

Galian laughed. It was not a laugh of humor though. It was a laugh of madnesss. "You think to speak of honor Beragon? Honor was a word from the world before. We no longer live in that world. Those that usurp the earth now do so with a hatred and vengeance our kin have never known and likely will never know. And it is for that reason we are all doomed. Our sun is setting and soon all we will know is darkness."

"Yes, liege. But surely there is hope? Surely there are things we can do. All has not been lost yet." Beragon said the words more to comfort himself and Galian knew this. Thus, he allowed him this small illusion of hope. Hope was a precious thing.

He turned back to the sea and watched the lightning dance among the clouds while the waves danced below.

"One more thing Sire."

Galian turned back to Beragon, "Yes?"

"We have a visitor. A stowaway that demands to see you. It was a ship that came in from Airendight a few hours ago. He claims he has important information for you, but more importantly he demands sanctuary."

"Sanctuary?"

"Yes, that is what he said."

   2.   Ending –

The castle lay in ruins.

Galian could make out the ramparts, their cobbled remains still rising up from the air but charred black from the fire that had ravaged the place the night before.

The bodies were still there, vultures picking among the remains, scavenging upon what dead were not too burned to provide nourishment, their flesh not burned away entirely.

He did not venture closer. He did not want to. It was too much to accept. He knew the people, his people, that lay among those remains and he sought to remember them as they were in life, not like this, not as torn and discarded lifeless dolls, playthings of the gods, terminated on the whim of a deity that had lost interest.

He could still see some of the Kramaj wandering among the ruins, scavenging just like the vultures, for anything that might be useable and that might be used to help them in their quest to eradicate all like him, to purge the world of him and his kind.

They were too busy in their search to bother looking upward to the ridge were he lay motionless, watching and waiting until they were gone and he could then begin the task of looking for survivors, knowing there would probably be none.

One queen lay dead. Arianna, the Queen of the Ruby Tresses was now falled and with her the ire of the gods upon the land itself had started. The rumblings deep within the earth he had felt. The prophecy would be fulfilled.

"God help them, they know not what they do." He muttered while remembering the words he was taught as a youth, the litany of things to come –

Ere when the queens shall fall
And the dark clouds loom below
Earth shall arise from slumber
And the times, they shall begin again
Fire, water and destruction
Shall rework the creation anew
From death will come life
From ending shall come beginning
As the old falls to be replaced anew
And the wheel turns ever on
Ever on and ever on."

He closed his eyes and hoped to sleep. And soon sleep came and there were no dreams and in the dark recesses of his mind he felt not peace but emptiness and nothingness, a peace of sorts for one whose world was collapsing around him.

Week 48
DESCRIPTION

Description is to writing what spice is to food or what color is to vision or what instruments are to music. The way a writer uses description is often his or her most defining characteristic. Whether the descriptions are sparse, such as those of Ernest Hemingway or elaborate and lush, like those of Anne Rice, the way a writer describes things will often set the tone and either endear or alienate the prospective reader. More importantly, our taste as a culture has changed over time and this too has affected what is acceptable in terms of description.

Description refers to the words we use to create an idea in the readers mind. Some readers will think verbally, some visually and most using a bit of both. Whatever senses the writer uses to ingest what we have written, it is important that we involve as many senses as possible in our description of a "thing". "Thing", in this sense of the word can mean concrete things such as a building, a person, a wreck or an apple or it can also mean more abstract things such as a feeling or a mood or a reaction. Description is probably the most powerful tool a writer can use to bring a story to life other than dialogue. This is because our most common interactions with the world take place through conversation or observation.

Why does description bring something to life? It does this because it provides "detail" in the form of word images which the reader is forced to associate with his own memory of these same words. Thus, each word used in a description helps the reader to bring more and more of his experience into the reading of the book and when this happens the book and the characters and places within it begin to take on form. We all remember the "Dick and Jane" stories from our early years of school. Often those books were absent all but the barest form of descriptions. Instead, the books offered pictures so that we could use our impressions and perceptions to bring the book to life. A picture book or a movie can do without word based descriptions since it recreates the experience in another format, by the action taking place on the page or the screen or in the case of the movie, by the sounds the viewer hears. Notice that in both of these forms we still "read" when we need to be told about a taste or a smell or a touch. This is because these forms of descriptions are not transmittable through either medium as of yet. Thus, this should help us understand that description is more than anything else a bridge to the artificial experience which allows us to recreate what we cannot participate in directly.

Descriptions can be elaborate and use simile and metaphor and analogy or they can be simple and use adverbs. Using metaphor, simile and analogy relies on our reader having the cultural background to understand such references and thus recreate the image/experience we have in mind when writing them. However, adverbs and other direct descriptions allow the reader to go back to his or her own experiences regardless of cultural experiences. One requires translation and the other does not. However, as readers we often value complex communication more so than the simple communication since it takes advantage of our cultural knowledge and experience.

Another way to think about description is as decoration. We can four homes all built exactly the same and end with four different environments depending on the individual or families living within them. This is because each will bring his or her or their own unique ideas of what an environment/home means to them. Thus, some will have a television and work out equipment in the same room that another person uses as a library and study area. The end result is two different experiences. Description can be used like this. We can think of the basic sentence without description as the baseline structure. Here in an example:

The cow jumped over the moon.

We can then modify this sentence to create different moods, experiences and perceptions depending on our objectives as a writer. We can make the sentence anxious:

The trembling cow felt fearful because it knew it could never make the jump over the moon. But try he did, and…..he made it!

We can make the sentence fearful:

The cow was halfway between the earth and the moon when he realized landing was going to be a problem. In fact, it would probably be the last problem he ever had. He thought of the pasture he would never see again as he quickly plummeted past the far side of the moon to the ground below where he finally hit with a loud splat.

The point is that a description gives life to the story. A description in this context is not necessarily just a word but it can also be a sentence or anything that adds to the readers experience and brings the story to life. As writers, we must always challenge ourselves to bring the stories to life and this means learning the art of good description. Thankfully, just like any art it is something you get better at with practice. Thus, the cow and I will continue working until we get it right!

WEEK 49
TENURE

How many of you would be willing to go out and do a heart operation on a whim? Not many of us. However, legions are the number of would-be-writers who dive into a novel or screenplay thinking they will be able to do just as good as someone who has spent ten years perfecting their craft and developing their skills. Why is this the case? Partly because we do all have an innate ability to tell stories. It is how we are born and what we naturally do in our lives day in and day out via everyday interaction. However, most of us know how to run and climb too but that doesn't mean we can go scale K-2 or run a marathon without preparation and training. Regardless of what most beginners think there is a great deal of learned skill involved in writing a novel or a screenplay. It is just like any other activity and requires time and effort to develop rudimentary skill into a talent strong enough to overcome the barriers to publication or production.

There have been various time frames put forth as gestation/training periods for a writer. Some say it takes five years from the first day of serious writing and some say ten years. The bottom line is that a new writer should AT LEAST expect to spend five to ten years doing nothing but grinding their wheels and learning the craft. Not only that but most writers will complete one to three novels and/or screenplays which are unpalatable or complete failures before they are able to complete a project of merit. Thus, expecting to go out and write your first novel or screenplay and turn around and sell it borders on the worst type of self-delusion when it comes to writing. It is simply a very difficult task to accomplish and those who do it are far and few between. We hear those stories because they ARE exceptions to the norm. If they were not they would never be worth telling.

So, considering the above, writing is not something to be taken lightly if your goal is publication and an income. Of course you can write for yourself and that is a perfectly reasonable and respectable goal that many writers choose. However, writing to please yourself is not the same type of undertaking as attempting to write for publication and establish a career as a writer. The latter takes far more effort, discipline and talent. These are all acquirable but they take time and effort or a significant period of time. A time period that in the end is about the same as mastering the skills necessary to perform heart surgery. So, stick with it but be prepared for a lot of work and a proper investment of time. Don't be deluded that success will come easy. Writing is just like anything else in life it takes time and effort.

WEEK 50
THE UNTALENTED WRITER

So you want to write a book? This was the same thought I have had for most of my life. As long as I remember I have always loved books and the way they can transform your life through the power of words. Like many people this love of books soon turned into a desire to write them. So like most with this desire I began what would end up being several failed attempts to write a book. In case you don't know, writing a book is not an easy endeavor. And that is simply writing ANY book. Writing a BAD book is not even easy. Writing a bad book takes considerable amounts of effort and persistence sustained over a long period of time. It goes without saying that writing a good book that a reader will enjoy requires much more in terms of talent, ingenuity, art and effort.

Once you have started on the journey of writing a book there comes a point where you realize that it is either working or it is not. If it is not working you then have to ask yourself why. The reasons may vary but the most frustrating reason is because your writing is simply not good enough. That is the death blow to any writing career. If your writing is not good enough then you are in serious trouble if you aspire to be a writer. This book is for people who find that to be the case. What to do and how to deal with it and in the end find success despite what seems to be insurmountable obstacles.

So what should you do once you have determined that the book you are writing is not any good?

1. Finish the book. No matter how bad the book is it is important that you finish it. Once you finish it at least you have something to work with. And it is after the first draft that the real work begins.
2. Read, Read, Read and then read some more. There is nothing that can replace the knowledge you get from reading well written books. It is the writer's best form

of education. It is what drove you to write in the first place. All writers are heavy readers.

3. Write much and write often. Any writing you do helps your craft. Therefore keeping a journal and doing daily exercises over and above the writing you do on your book is very important. Every word you write builds skill and helps you to develop your style.
4. Start another book and finish it.
5. Do it all over again.

After many repetitions of this formula you will eventually be able to write a decent book. Or at least you should be able to. If you fail in doing this then you are in trouble because this is the last resort.

Let's discuss some general guidelines you should use in writing a novel.

1) First of all you should have a model in mind. A model is a novel that you have read that is similar to the one you have in mind. This keeps you from swimming without a rope so to speak. When you are in trouble you can look to your model to see how that author handled it and then you will be on your way to finishing the book. All beginning writers should use a model. If you like the style and the way the writer writes then even try to copy that. It will be a useful practice for your first novel. Every writer should have a model at first.

2) Second of all you should be writing a story that you love. Find something you are very passionate about. It is only the passion that will sustain you through to the end of a novel length work. Anything less will fall short. Therefore, find a subject that excites and enthralls you. One that you are eager to write about.

3) Third, plot out your novel scene by scene from the beginning to the end before you ever begin writing. This will ensure that you don't get stuck. If you do get stuck you can simply go to another scene that you find more interesting and write it. Or if

need be an easier scene. Bottom line is that this approach will ensure that you finish the book.

4) Fourthly, don't go back and read what you have written until the book is finished. If you go back and read it somewhere along the way it will discourage you and you will be unlikely to finish it. And it is very important that you finish the first draft. Only with a first draft in hand can you look forward to completing a respectable book.

These guidelines should get you through the first draft of the book. When you complete the first draft return to this document.

WEEK 51
A CHARACTER ANDA PROBLEM

When it boils down to it, fiction writing is about two things – a character and a problem. The task of the fiction writer is to make the reader care about the character – or at the least be intrigued enough by him to want to see how he handles the problem and to make the problem important and interesting enough to engage the reader. If the writer can accomplish these two things then he or she has done the minimum necessary to write a novel. Of course, going above and beyond this is required to write a novel that the reader will remember. Even more is required to make the novel one for the ages. However, everything else that can be done goes into enhancing one of these two facets of the novel. Even the setting is in essence either an extension of the character and/or the problem.

Given the above, what is that makes a reader read. What creates a memorable or even transcendent experience? Essentially, the closer a reader feels to the reader or the problem – the more affinity there is – the more intense and involving will be the reading experience. This is why some books will appeal to some people and other books will appeal to other people. No book appeals to everyone simply because no two people share the same experiences or outlook in life. But for certain, if a writer writes from the heart and stays true to their own experiences and outlook they are assured of eventually finding someone – even if only one person – who can relate to that experience and enjoy the book or at the least get something from it. This is providing of course that it is written comprehensibly and follows the basic rules of writing.

Thus, in the end the only thing a writing teacher can teach is how to translate their experiences and their outlooks into fiction on a very basic level. Once a writer is able to do this it is up to that individual to find a story or a character that speaks through them and allows for an involving experience. Most often, the first attempt to do this will be unsuccessful. It will be unsuccessful because just like anything else, good writing takes practice. In the end there is usually one of two possible problems, rarely both. Either the story is not interesting and generally unworkable or the writing masks an otherwise attractive story. By far, the better of the two problems is the good story with bad writing.

The writer's journey is a long one, to be sure. It is one fraught with frustration and temptations to give up and forget the entire notion of writing. It is one that will lead to many cases of rejection and criticism. But even with those pitfalls it is perhaps one of the most rewarding journeys a human being can take in this world. After all, the writer in some sense does defy the laws of mortality. Regardless of what happens to the writer, the words will live on if they have reached an audience and in the end this is all we can ask for – as writers, and as human being.

Week 52
WRITING AS A PROCESS

Writing is like painting or gardening – you never really finish and even when you think you are there is usually something you can find that needs more work. The key to good writing is to continue to work at it until YOU are satisfied. The most important thing to remember is that in the end you have to please yourself above all else. Hopefully, your artistic vision is in line with a decent number of other people – if so then you should have a good sell through, if not then…. Can you write for pure profit? Yes, of course you can and in the end all writers do this to make ends meet. Writing is not a profession of the rich. The John Grisham's and Sandra Brown's are rare. More common is the individual who writes for the love of it but must maintain a secondary job regardless.

Despite the above, writing is one of the most rewarding and soul enhancing experiences an individual can pursue. It allows one to reflect on life, try to find some meaning in the process of it and create experiences that enrich the lives of others. This itself is enough to justify the pursuit of writing and art in general. For, in the end writing is art and art is never perfect but instead it is like nature – messy, wildly creative and it requires a little bit of madness to do right.

A writer is born in the sense that a writer feels the need to express. They must express their life experiences in some form or fashion. Cultivating what it takes to simply write into a career of some substance is usually a life long endeavor. However, if one can do it then it offers satisfaction and sustenance beyond the norm in the world of work and toil. Above all remember that a career is not built in a day and that as long as you can do your work daily, write one story/novel/article after another and continually approve then you will eventually arrive at the place you want to go. It requires hard work, persistence and above all dedication. If you have these qualities then nothing can stop you as long as you always work to improve.

Good luck and happy writing!

THE END

FURTHER REFERENCES

Below are the various books I have used in my own education
and which other writers might find helpful.   I have listed them
in order of inspiration using my own form.

Story by Robert Mckee, Reganbooks: Harper Collins. ISBN 0-
06-039168-5.

Plot & Structure by James Scott Bell, Writer's Digest Books.
ISBN 1-58297-294-X.

The Analysis of Play Construction and Dramatic Principle
by W.T. Price, W.T. Price Publisher. (Circa. 1908, No ISBN).

Novelist's Essential Guide to Crafting Scenes by Raymond
Obstfeld, Writer's Digest Books. ISBN 0-89879-973-2.

Novelist's Essential Guide to Creating Plot by J. Madison
Davis, Writer's Digest Books. ISBN 0-89879-984-8.

The Way of the Storyteller by Ruth Sawyer, The Viking Press.
(Circa 1942, No ISBN).

Writing A Great Movie by Jeff Kitchen, Jeff Kitchen,
Publisher. ISBN 0-9747715-1-1.

The Courage to Write by Ralph Keyes, Henry Holt, Publisher.
ISBN 0-8050-3189-8.